THE UNITED NATIONS

AND

THE SUPERPOWERS

CONSULTING EDITOR:

Inis L. Claude, Jr.

STUDIES IN POLITICAL SCIENCE

The
United Nations
and the
Superpowers

United States—Soviet Interaction
at the United Nations

SECOND EDITION

JOHN G. STOESSINGER
Hunter College • The City University of New York

with the assistance of
ROBERT G. McKELVEY

RANDOM HOUSE   NEW YORK

TO

INIS L. CLAUDE, JR.

PREFACE TO
THE SECOND EDITION

This book has a threefold purpose: to study the dynamics of the United States–Soviet relationship at the UN; to point up the effects of this relationship on the development of the United Nations itself; and to evaluate the significance of this development for the future of superpower relations with the Organization.

Our approach is not general and exhaustive, but highly selective. We have chosen nine cases of superpower interaction, and divided them into three groups.

Part I is a study of the superpowers' effect on the political and constitutional evolution of the three key UN organs: the Security Council, the General Assembly, and the Office of the Secretary-General. The first case focuses on the superpowers and the Security Council veto. We seek to discover how many of the 105 Soviet vetoes have actually prevented further UN action. How has the Organization circumvented Soviet vetoes and how have these circumventions affected the distribution of power among the UN organs? We seek to explain the "hidden" American veto and what effect it has had on the UN. The second case deals with the changing membership of the General Assembly. Why were only nine states permitted to join the UN during its first ten years, whereas more than sixty joined during the past decade? What were the political effects on the superpowers of the decade of exclusion and the later decade of rapid entry? The problem of Chinese representation is singled out as a good example of the way in which the superpowers, particularly the United States, had to adapt their tactics to the changing General Assembly. The third case, which compares the American attack on the Office of the Secretary-General in the early 1950's with the Soviet assault a decade later, reveals a great deal about the attitudes of the superpowers toward the UN chief executive and the international civil service.

In Part II we analyze the major UN efforts in peace-keeping. There the Organization has been interposed between the clashing national interests of the superpowers. Our first case study analyzes the superpower confrontations during the Middle East crises of 1956 and 1967 and the birth and death of the UN Emergency Force (UNEF). The second case assesses the shifting U.S.–Soviet attitudes toward the UN Operation in the Congo (ONUC) during the four-year crisis. The third case deals with the financial implications of these two peace forces, which not only threatened to bankrupt the UN but created a major political and constitutional crisis. In all three cases, we have traced the UN's quest for common ground between the superpowers' antithetical interests on deeply divisive issues.

Part III analyzes superpower behavior in three selected problem areas in the economic and social realm. The first case focuses on the superpowers' roles in creating and subsequently undoing the International Refugee Organization; the second analyzes the U.S.–Soviet interaction that created the International Atomic Energy Agency, only to cripple it later; and the final case looks into the superpower struggle over a Special Fund project in Cuba in 1963. These cases reveal clearly that the national-interest considerations that dominated the peace-keeping operations analyzed in Part II also affected the UN's economic and social activities.

The over-all purpose of this book is not to present another review of the development of UN institutions over the past twenty-five years. Our objective is to focus on those trends from the Organization's past which, it appears to us, are going to dominate its future. Such a task led us to concentrate our attention on the interaction of the superpowers at the United Nations.

Briefly, the major points of our position may be summarized as follows. During the past twenty-five years, both superpowers have tried to use the UN as a vehicle for the advancement of their individual, antithetical foreign-policy interests. In this quest, the Organization has been a more important vehicle for the United States than for the Soviet Union, because the United States has successfully involved the UN in more activities that have served its national interest. The UN has often been persuaded to do collectively what the United States might have had to do individually. This has been true for a number of reasons, including the important fact that the objectives of United States policy have been more compatible with the UN Charter than those of the Soviet Union. No less important, however, has been the fact that, for most of its history, the UN has been controlled politically and financially by the United States and its military allies. On the several occasions when UN action threatened U.S. national interests, the United States reacted vigorously—by casting "hidden" vetoes, infringing on the neutrality of the Secretariat, crippling a UN agency through outside bilateral agreements, and embarking on similar courses of action that are analyzed in detail in the text. Such actions, however, have been relatively infrequent, not because the United States neglected its national interest, but because the UN majority generally cared so well for it.

It is our belief that recent changes in the United Nations, particularly in membership, indicate that the U.S. honeymoon is over. The presence of more than 120 nations in the General Assembly, compared with 60 in 1954 or even 82 in 1959, means—to pick one example—that the United States and its allies have lost the two-thirds majority that is necessary for the passage of important resolutions. In the past, the United States—certain of its automatic majority—could advocate majority diplomacy without fear. Today, United States diplomats will have to work harder and make more compromises if they are to continue to build winning coalitions. And these compromises must be struck not with traditional political and cultural allies, as in the past, but with the new Afro-Asian majority, which has different sets of needs and interests. In extreme circumstances, the United States may actually have to use "absolute weapons," such as the veto power, to protect vital national interests. If past performance is any guide, the United States will not adjust easily to its new position. It is possible that, accustomed to having its way for so long, it may precipitate a crisis that will undermine the Organization, or Congress and public opinion may become sufficiently disenchanted to force a sharp cut in American support of the UN. We feel that the late Ambassador Adlai E. Stevenson was correct when he stated that "the crisis of our loyalty to the United Nations [was] still ahead of us." It is our hope that our consideration of the background of this forthcoming crisis of conscience will contribute to a discussion that will enable the United States to deal more wisely with it.

The lessons of the past quarter century also show some grounds for optimism. To some, it may appear that because it has been so deeply involved in power politics and the national-interest struggles between the superpowers, the United Nations has been a failure. The most important conclusion of this book is that such a view is wrong. While it is true that many of the UN's difficulties have their origin in the East-West conflict, it is our belief that the Organization has gained in strength by being involved instead of seeking a quieter place on the sidelines. In this role, the UN has been bent first one way, then another, as the superpowers attempted to use it, often against each other. But on balance, our study suggests that the UN's strength and influence have grown not only in spite of superpower conflict, but also *because* of it. In today's world, the price of relevance for the United Nations is conflict. The struggle toward order finds its nourishment in the same soil as the struggle for power.

Work on this book was begun six years ago, largely in response to the growing disenchantment with the UN that I found among government officials, colleagues, and students. I acknowledge gratefully the valuable research assistance of Mr. Ralph Hellmold of Columbia University during preparation of the first draft, particularly on Chapters 2, 3, 5, and 9, and of Miss Marcia Rosenfeld, also of Columbia University, for her help on Chapter 1. Both are absolved entirely of any errors of fact or other shortcomings of this book. During work on the final draft, I enjoyed the collaboration of Mr. Robert G. McKelvey of Columbia University, who rendered valuable research assistance on each chapter of the book. He also shared his ideas with the author, particularly on the relationship of the superpowers' national interests to the UN's evolution, and helped to reshape the book along these lines. For this reason he shares partial responsibility with me for the final product. For permission to adapt for this volume passages from some of my previously published works, I am also grateful to the University of Minnesota Press, publishers of *The Refugee and the World Community* (1956); The Brookings Institution, publishers of *Financing the United Nations System* (1964); and New York University

Press, publishers of *Organizing Peace in the Nuclear Age* (1953), in which appeared my article "Atoms-for-Peace: The International Atomic Energy Agency."

Finally, it is my privilege to express my appreciation to the man who first aroused my interest in the United Nations as a political institution: Inis L. Claude, Jr.

J. G. S.

CONTENTS

INTRODUCTION

In this book, Professor John G. Stoessinger depicts with great clarity and accuracy the role of the two superpowers—the United States and the Soviet Union—during the whole of the life of the United Nations. A central feature of the United Nations Charter, the arrangements for collective measures based upon the presumed unanimity of the great powers soon became a dead letter. The cold war took the place of a united great power front in support of peace. A growing malaise, aggravated by profound ideological differences, conditioned the relationships between the United States and the Soviet Union in the United Nations.

It could easily be regarded a matter of astonishment that the United Nations should survive this major rupture between the superpowers, but survive it did, and indeed, on certain critical occasions even blunted the edges of the rivalry. Although the United Nations was the conspicuous and most highly publicized arena of the cold war, through the powerful weaponry of quiet diplomacy, it sometimes nudged the great powers out of critical and highly explosive situations.

Professor Stoessinger describes the sweep of this rivalry as it affected the work of principal organs of the United Nations and either forestalled the prospect of agreement on major issues before the organization or compelled it to resort to special types of improvisation, particularly in the peace-keeping field. He describes the heavy strains placed upon the organization as a result of these deeply set differences, but also indicates that the organization derived strength from the rivalry. In a real sense, these continuing storms contributed to the seaworthiness and strength of the organization. The smaller powers and the Secretary-General found themselves under the almost continuous necessity of filling the serious voids caused by superpower rivalry. The smaller powers often provided both the personnel and the resources necessary for effective action in peace-keeping operations, and the membership depended increasingly upon the Secretary-General to serve both as a catalyst and as an operational executive. If great power unity had prevailed, it is certain that the role of the third powers and the Secretary-General would have been less conspicuous and more subordinate.

Although the major theme of the book is an assessment of the rivalries of the superpowers and their impact upon the constitutional and political life of the United Nations, stress is also properly placed upon the separate interests and attitudes of the two superpowers toward the United Nations. In the McCarthy era of the early fifties, the Secretariat was buffeted by heavy attacks from official Washington and from powerful elements in the American public, but with this exception, the United States maintained a scrupulous respect for the role and status of the Secretariat and supported it in its activities. The Soviet Union was never content with its role in the Secretariat nor with the Secretariat's role in the Organization. It believed the Secretariat should confine itself primarily to the servicing of conferences and avoid an executive role in peace-keeping operations. The Soviet Government broke with both Trygve Lie and Dag Hammarskjöld for somewhat different reasons, but both men engaged in active roles in major peace-keeping operations, the policies of which ran contrary to the Soviet interest.

Professor Stoessinger's selection of nine case studies is admirable and covers the main spectrum of superpower rivalries and of their separate interests and attitudes toward the United Nations. Although all organs of the United Nations felt the impact of the rivalry, the Security Council, the General Assembly, and the Secretariat provided the main focuses for the tension which cast its shadow on the whole Organization.

The analyses of the Suez crises, of the Congo crisis, and of the ensuing political, constitutional, and financial difficulties in the United Nations cover the major thread in the United Nations story; the treatment of human rights, atoms for peace, and Cuba and the Special Fund throws much-needed light on superpower attitudes toward these areas of substance and operational activities.

The concluding chapter is a succinct analysis and summary of the major fields and causes of tension between the superpowers.

The book is an invaluable contribution to the literature of the United Nations and should command the interest of many readers.

ANDREW W. CORDIER, *Columbia University*

PART I

The Superpowers and the Constitutional Evolution of the United Nations

CHAPTER 1

---•◦•---

The Security Council: The Veto and the Superpowers

The United States Government would not remain one day in the United Nations without retaining the veto power.
Cordell Hull
U.S. Secretary of State, 1944.

The veto power is the paramount principle which constitutes the cornerstone of the United Nations.
Andrei Y. Vishinsky
Soviet Delegate to the
United Nations, 1950.

One of the more persistent myths surrounding the United Nations concerns the use of the veto power by the Soviet Union and the United States. It is an established fact that by 1969 the Soviet Union had vetoed 105 Security Council resolutions, whereas the United States had yet to cast its first veto. Hence, it is said that the Soviet Union's frequent use of the veto has hampered and weakened the United Nations by preventing it from acting, while the United States has exercised remarkable self-discipline by never using the veto at all.

This chapter will show that neither part of this myth is accurate. On the one hand, the ultimate effect of the Soviet veto on UN action has been considerably exaggerated. On the other, while it is technically correct to say that the United States has never cast a veto, we shall see that the United States has, in fact, developed a "hidden veto," which it has used frequently and effectively. In short, it is one thesis of this chapter that the difference in the behavior of the superpowers on the use of the veto is more apparent than real; both have tried to protect their national interests, although by different parliamentary tactics. Moreover, we shall attempt to show that the interaction between the superpowers on the veto has not necessarily had a negative effect on the development of the United Nations. On the contrary, the United Nations has responded to the challenge with imagination and flexibility, and this response has led to important constitutional and political changes within the Organization. One reason why the United Nations today is a different—and stronger—organization from the one established in 1945 has been its ability to rise to the challenge of the superpower veto.

The framers of the Charter gave the Security Council extensive powers to keep the peace. The Council was to consist of eleven members, five of which—the United States, the Soviet Union, Great Britain, France, and China—were to be permanent. In addition, six nonpermanent members were to be elected by the General Assembly for two-year terms. The Charter empowered the Security Council to recommend means of peaceful settlement of disputes; and, if a nation committed an act of aggression, the Council was to have the power to apply sanctions against the aggressor. Such sanctions might range from the severance of diplomatic relations all the way to collective military action.

The Big Five were clearly intended to dominate the Council. It was hoped that no aggressor would then be able to challenge such an overwhelming agglomeration of power. The Big Five, in return for their primary responsibility to keep the peace, received commensurate privileges: a permanent seat on the Council and the veto power, by which each of the Big Five could prevent the Security Council from taking action on a substantive issue. Three of the Great powers at San Francisco—the United States, the Soviet Union, and Great Britain—insisted on the right of veto and none of them would have acceded to the United Nations without it. China and France at first took a more flexible position, but the rigid stand of the Big Three soon resulted in their equally firm insistence on the veto rule.

The exact wording of Article 27 of the Charter, which established the veto power, is as follows:

1. Each member of the Security Council shall have one vote.
2. Decisions of the Security Council on procedural matters shall be made by an affirmative vote of seven members.

3. Decisions of the Security Council on all other matters shall be made by an affirmative vote of seven members including the concurring votes of the permanent members; provided that in decisions under Chapter VI, and under paragraph 3 of Article 52, a party to a dispute shall abstain from voting.

While a major power was required to abstain from voting on resolutions related to the peaceful settlement of disputes to which it was a party, it was technically free to veto all other nonprocedural matters. In addition, the powers agreed that the decision whether a matter was substantive or procedural was itself a substantive question and hence subject to veto. Thus, by a double veto system —one veto to decide whether the issue was substantive or procedural and the second on the issue itself—a Great Power could veto anything it chose, with the single exception of questions regarding the peaceful settlement of disputes to which it was a party. Or, to put it the other way round, all the Great Powers had to be in agreement before the Security Council could act. Clearly, it seemed that close cooperation among the Big Five would be a necessary prerequisite for an effective Security Council. Yet, the deepening split between the superpowers and the 9 vetoes cast by the Soviet Union during 1946 adumbrated to many observers a succession of paralyzing vetoes that could jeopardize the effectiveness of the entire United Nations.

In January 1966, the Security Council was enlarged from eleven to fifteen members. The four new nonpermanent members were all to be selected from the new nations of the world. An affirmative vote by the Council now required 9 votes rather than 7. The veto power of the Big Five remained unaffected by the Charter amendment.

The Soviet Union and the Veto

The Soviet Union has been responsible for 105 of the 113 vetoes cast by 1969, or over 90 percent of the total. But the figures themselves do not adequately explain the picture. One must see what effect the vetoes had on the United Nations *after* they were cast.

A Soviet veto could meet one of three different fates. First, it could "stick" completely, meaning that no significant further action on the vetoed issue was taken by other organs of the United Nations or by states outside the United Nations. For example, the Soviet veto of an investigation of the Indian invasion of Goa "stuck." Second, a veto could be "circumvented" if another organ of the United Nations provided alternative machinery. In some cases, this alternative machinery could continue the effective direction of the action in place of the paralyzed Security Council. For example, the General Assembly effectively circumvented the Soviet vetoes cast during the Korean War by directing the "police action" itself. In other cases, the United Nations could try another approach, but still fail to resolve the issue. For example, in 1954 the Soviet Union vetoed a resolution requesting Egypt to lift its blockade of Israeli shipping through the Suez Canal and referring the dispute to the Egyptian-Israeli Mixed Armistice Commission for negotiation. Despite the veto, Secretary-General Hammarskjöld met with the Egyptians and reached an agreement that, in effect, would have permitted Israeli cargoes to pass through the Canal. At the last moment, however, the Egyptian government changed its mind and the arrangement fell through. But the important point is that it was *not* the veto that prevented the successful resolution of the issue. The Secretary-General's Office had provided adequate alternatives, but the issue remained unresolved because of the action of one of the states directly involved. Thus, our criterion of a circumvented veto is not necessarily the successful settlement of an issue but the capacity of the United Nations to provide alternative machinery to fill the breach left by a paralyzed Security Council. As a third fate, a veto may be superseded either because the disputants negotiated the issue directly, as happened in the Berlin Blockade, or because changing circumstances may resolve the dispute, as when the Soviet Union decided not to protect Iraq's claim to Kuwait after a pro-Western government had taken power in Iraq. In sum, therefore, a Soviet veto can "stick," be circumvented, or be superseded.

In general, one can distinguish four major areas in which the USSR has used the veto to protect and promote its national interest: vetoes cast in direct U.S.–Soviet confrontations; vetoes cast on behalf of a Communist ally; vetoes cast on behalf of a state outside the Communist bloc; and vetoes cast against candidates for UN membership. Let us now examine in greater detail the consequences of Soviet vetoes in each of these.

The Soviet Union has used the veto eighteen times to protect its national interest in a direct clash with the United States.[1] It vetoed 5 resolutions calling for UN action in such cold-war confrontations as the Berlin Blockade, the Hungarian Revolution, the destruction of a U.S. RB-47 airplane (2 vetoes), and the Czechoslovak crisis of 1968. The USSR twice vetoed the election of a Secretary-General whom the United States favored strongly. It also vetoed five measures related to disarmament and cast 6 vetoes at various points during the UN Operation in the Congo.

Not all of these vetoes have prevented further UN action. When the General Assembly voted to extend the term of Secretary-General Trygve Lie during the Korean War, it circumvented one Soviet veto. When the Soviet Union vetoed an American draft resolution on the Hungarian crisis, an emergency session of the General Assembly passed a more strongly worded resolution recommending that the Secretary-General investigate the situation and suggest methods of ending the foreign intervention. Neither the Secretary-General nor a Special Committee appointed by him could secure the cooperation of the new Soviet-sponsored government in Hungary and thus the matter was eventually dropped. From the UN point of view, however, the immediate cause of failure was not the Soviet veto. The Organization did develop compensatory if somewhat token machinery, but the attitude of the Hungarian government prevented further action. The 6 vetoes cast during the Congo Operation were all circumvented. The vetoed proposals were enacted by the Assembly in similar if not always identical language and the basic objective of the USSR—the obstruction of the Congo Operation—was not achieved. Two further issues which elicited Soviet vetoes —the Berlin Blockade and the RB-47 incident—were resolved through negotiation between the superpowers without direct UN involvement. The remaining 7 vetoes, however, did stick and no further action was taken inside or outside the world organization.

A second group of 16 vetoes was cast by the Soviet Union not to protect itself directly, but to assist a Communist ally. By vetoing two resolutions the USSR prevented a UN inquiry into the new

Communist government in Czechoslovakia in 1948. One veto on behalf of Albania over the Corfu Channel dispute with Great Britain was resolved outside the United Nations by an agreement of the parties to submit the issue to the International Court of Justice. Another veto—on behalf of North Vietnam against Thailand's charge of Communist infiltration—was superseded by changed circumstances. The Soviet Union vetoed five resolutions during the Korean War, but these vetoes, like those cast during the Congo Operation, did not prevent the United Nations from achieving its basic objectives. Six vetoes cast to protect Greece's Communist northern neighbors during the Greek Civil War were effectively circumvented by General Assembly action. Finally, a Soviet veto on a resolution concerning the overthrow of the Communist government in Guatemala in 1954 was superseded. In sum, only the 2 vetoes cast over Czechoslovakia were final; 11 others were circumvented by UN action; and 3 were bypassed by events outside the United Nations.[2]

Sixteen vetoes cast by the Soviet Union may be described as proxy vetoes or vetoes cast on behalf of neutralist states with which the USSR wished to gain favor.[3] Eleven of these were used on behalf of Arab states against former colonial powers or against Israel. Four of them—1 on the diversion of the river Jordan and 3 cast at various points in the continuing Syrian-Israeli dispute—were final.

The very first veto in the Security Council was cast in 1946 against a resolution expressing confidence that the British and French would withdraw their forces from Syria and Lebanon. This veto was superseded outside the United Nations as the two powers expressed their intention to withdraw and did so promptly. Another pro-Arab veto was also superseded outside the United Nations when the USSR refused to support Iraq's claim to Kuwait. The remaining 4 pro-Arab vetoes were all circumvented by UN action. Two of the 4 were cast on behalf of Egypt. One vetoed resolution concerned the passage of Israeli cargoes through the Suez Canal. As noted above, Secretary-General Hammarskjöld reached an agreement with the Egyptian government, but at the last moment the scheme failed. The second pro-Egyptian veto was cast in 1956 against a resolution calling on Egypt, the United Kingdom, and

France to continue their negotiations and for Egypt to submit guarantees that the Canal would be managed effectively. Despite the veto, the talks continued under the guidance of the Secretary-General. When the Canal was reopened in April 1957, Egypt deposited an instrument with the United Nations acknowledging its treaty obligations under international law and later accepted the jurisdiction of the International Court of Justice on matters of interpretation.

Two Soviet vetoes were cast during the Lebanon crisis of 1958, and both were circumvented by General Assembly action.

Three of the vetoes by proxy were used on behalf of India. The first, on the Kashmir problem, stuck. A second veto on Kashmir, cast against fuller negotiations, was bypassed when the United States succeeded in bringing India and Pakistan together for talks in exchange for U.S. aid to India during the Chinese invasion of that country. The third, on Goa, struck. Finally, 2 vetoes cast over Indonesian independence were circumvented by Assembly action, but a veto cast in the 1964 Indonesian-Malaysian dispute has stuck. In sum, therefore, 7 proxy vetoes for neutralist states have stuck; 6 were circumvented by UN action; and 3 were superseded by outside circumstances.

The largest number of vetoes, 51, was used to block the admission of new members to the United Nations. This total, however, is not as staggering as it appears, since 34 of these 51 vetoes were "repeats." Italy, for example, was vetoed 6 times, and Portugal, Jordan, Ireland, Ceylon, South Korea, South Vietnam, and Japan were vetoed 4 times each. One Soviet objective in vetoing the admission of these states was to force the United States to admit such Communist states as Albania, Bulgaria, Hungary, and Rumania to the world organization. In an effort to break this membership deadlock, the two superpowers negotiated directly and in 1955 reached agreement on a "package deal" that made possible the admission of sixteen new members, including most of the protégés of both superpowers. In one sense, therefore, the Soviet vetoes attained their end: the admission of the Communist applicants. But in another sense, they were superseded, since all the U.S. candidates against which vetoes had been cast—save South Korea and South Vietnam—were also admitted to membership. A decision of the superpowers taken outside the United Nations effectively resolved the membership stalemate. In all, forty-three of the membership vetoes were superseded by the "package deal" and only eight—four against South Vietnam and four against South Korea—have stuck.[4]

Four early Soviet vetoes—in 1946 against Spain—do not fit into any of the above categories, but their fate is clear.[5] They were cast in order to obtain more severe action against the Franco regime for its association with the Axis during World War II. While the Assembly passed resolutions similar to some of the vetoed proposals, the rapid development of the cold war and Spain's increasing value to the West prevented further action. In effect, these vetoes were superseded by changing circumstances.

The following table presents the above material in summary form.

SOVIET VETOES 1946–1969

	Stuck	Circumvented	Superseded	Total
Direct Confrontations	7 (39%)	8 (44%)	3 (17%)	18
For Communist Allies	2 (12%)	11 (69%)	3 (19%)	16
Proxy Vetoes	7 (44%)	6 (38%)	3 (18%)	16
Membership Vetoes	8 (16%)	—	43 (84%)	51
Spanish Question	—	—	4	4
	24 (23%)	25 (24%)	56 (53%)	105

An analysis of the table suggests several conclusions. First, it is a startling fact that nearly 80 percent of the Soviet Union vetoes have been rendered less effective in one way or another and 24 percent have been circumvented by action of the United Nations itself. The "circumventability" of a veto depends on several factors. The identity of the veto's beneficiary is of great importance and often determines the degree of political incentive to override a veto or the degree of political caution against such action. The legal-constitutional situation may also play an important part. Here one must ask how rigid the Charter is on a given point. On the membership question, for example, the Charter seems to exclude circumvention. Some states toyed with the idea, but the World Court refused to go along with their scheme. Then, there is a point at which the legal and political issues meet: given some latitude in the constitution and the political desire to circumvent a veto, is it *politically* possible to exploit the *constitutional* possibility? The Indian "liberation" of Goa is a case in point. The Soviet veto stuck in this case not because there was no alternative machinery that might have been used against it—the General Assembly could have served—but because it was clear that, in voting terms, the Assembly would have endorsed the Soviet position. The United States believed, probably correctly, that the Assembly would have supported the Soviet view of "liberation," not the Western view of "aggression." Hence, the veto served in this case as an instrument of the majority view in the United Nations rather than a device for blocking the majority position.

A second general conclusion emerging from our table concerns the Soviet vetoes that have stuck. The Soviet Union has been more successful in direct confrontations with the United States (39 percent) and in proxy vetoes cast on behalf of neutralist states (44 percent) than in vetoes on behalf of Communist allies (12 percent). In short, along with its own direct national interest, the USSR has been better able to protect the interests of neutrals than those of allies.

It is clear from the above that, in direct superpower confrontations, the United States and other UN members acknowledge the power realities of the situation. Pushing the United Nations too far in situations like the Hungarian Revolution or the Czechoslovak crisis, for example, runs the risk of shattering it altogether. The durable character of the proxy vetoes has also been an expression of cold-war realities: first, the United States has been reluctant to seek to upset a veto cast on behalf of a neutralist state, since, like the Soviet Union, it is anxious to win neutralist support. Moreover, the political realities noted above would make it difficult to mobilize a majority for such circumvention in the General Assembly. On the other hand, the United States has taken a strong interest in circumventing vetoes cast on behalf of Communist allies when the American national interest has been at stake. The five circumvented vetoes during the Korean War were cases in point. In all instances, the attitude of the two superpowers has been crucial to the durability of the veto.

A third general conclusion from the record suggests that the 105 vetoes have not constituted as formidable an obstacle to the solution of international problems as one might expect. In the first place, this total is somewhat misleading, since 34 of the membership vetoes were "repeats." More important, however, is the fact that in nearly 80 percent of the cases in which a veto had been cast, some further action was forthcoming. In 53 percent of the vetoed cases, the issues were settled outside the United Nations by direct negotiations or changing circumstances. Even in these cases however, the United Nations sometimes played a "good-offices" role. For example, the preliminary discussions about lifting the Berlin Blockade were held between Soviet and American officials at the United Nations.

The significant fact is that 24 percent of the vetoed issues, including important peace and security operations, were circumvented directly by compensatory UN action. In these instances, the USSR paralyzed the Security Council, but not the United Nations *in toto*. General Assembly action, as in the extension of Secretary-General Lie's term in 1950, and joint action by the Assembly and the Secretary-General, as in the Congo Operation, have been the major forms of UN compensatory machinery.

On balance, the evidence suggests that the United Nations, far from being helpless in the face of the Soviet veto, has responded to the challenge with imagination and flexibility. It has moved cautiously when the direct interest of a superpower has been at stake. In four-fifths of the cases, however, either the United Nations has been able to devise means to circumvent the veto, although not necessarily to solve the problem, or the issue has been effectively settled by outside events. In short, the veto has not been an insurmountable obstacle to the resolution of international issues.

Before considering the United States and the veto, it is interesting to note the fate of vetoes cast by members other than the Soviet Union: 4 by France, 3 by Great Britain, and 1 by China.[6] All of these were either circumvented by UN action or superseded by events. The creation of the United Nations Emergency Force by

the General Assembly in 1956 after British and French vetoes paralyzed the Security Council is a well-known case in point.

The United States and the Veto

The companion myth to the paralyzing Soviet veto is that of American self-denial. Western observers never tire of pointing out that the
United States has never used the veto. Some observers go so far as
to question whether the United States ever favored the inclusion
of the veto power in the UN Charter. Even so well-informed a
statesman as Senator John Sherman Cooper, former Ambassador to
India, asked in 1954 whether it was not true that the United
States, at the time of the approval of the Charter, "was opposed
to the veto."[7]

To assert that the United States objected to the inclusion of the
veto power is incorrect. To say that the United States has never
used the veto power is literally correct, but highly misleading in a
broader sense. The implication would be that one superpower had
selfishly put national interest above international considerations
while the other had unselfishly subordinated national interests in
order to further international cooperation. The fact of the matter is
that the United States has not used the veto because it has been
able to protect and promote its national interest in other ways.
By obtaining majority votes against resolutions it opposes, the United
States has never been forced to cast a veto. The key to this American
"hidden veto" has, of course, been the composition of the Security
Council. It is a fact that until the enlargement of the Council from
eleven to fifteen in 1966, a majority of its members usually were
military allies of the United States. In 1958, Premier Khrushchev
lashed out against what, in his view, was clear American domination of the Council:

> It is common knowledge that the majority in the Security
> Council is composed of the votes of countries dependent, in
> one way or another, primarily economically, on the USA.
> Thus, the Security Council in its present composition cannot
> be regarded as an impartial arbiter, and that is why it has
> of late ceased to play the important role in the maintenance

of international peace and security which devolved upon it by virtue of the United Nations Charter.[8]

When Khrushchev made this statement, eight votes on the Council were controlled by military allies of the United States in NATO and SEATO. Two members—Iraq and Sweden—were neutral in the East-West struggle. In the following year, Sweden was replaced by Italy, a member of NATO, and Iraq by Tunisia, another neutral.

Thus, in 1959, the United States had good reason to expect nine of the eleven Security Council members to support its position on any major East-West issue. As Norman J. Padelford has pointed out:

> It is clear from the record that when the Soviet Union finds its vital interests at stake there are now no other great powers generally inclined to stand with it. Therefore, the negative vote of the Soviet delegate usually becomes a sole veto, accompanied ordinarily by the vote of whatever satellite holds a non-permanent seat on the Council. When other great powers, particularly the United States and Great Britain, find their national interests at issue they can usually persuade other permanent members to go along with them either in casting a multiple negative vote sufficient to stop a proposal without the stigma of exercising a sole veto (or near-sole veto), or to join in introducing and passing a resolution more suitable to their desires.[9]

There are numerous cases on record which suggest that the United States has used its considerable influence to persuade members of the Council to form a negative majority for its position and thus avoid having to cast a veto. For example, during the protracted controversy over the admission of new members, the United States repeatedly blocked the admission of Soviet-sponsored candidates, not by a veto, but by prevailing upon its allies to back its position. The USSR, on the other hand, had to cast fifty-one vetoes to block American-sponsored candidates. The U-2 episode in 1960 was another typical case of the American "hidden veto" in action. In May of that year, the Soviet Union brought the case before the Security Council and introduced a resolution branding the flights by American planes over Soviet territory as "acts of aggression." Two states—the USSR and Poland—voted in favor of the Soviet motion; seven states voted against: Argentina, China, Ecuador, France, Italy, the United Kingdom, and the United States—all members of the Western alliance system. Two neutralist states—Ceylon and Tunisia—abstained.

This pattern began to change somewhat in 1966, when four nonpermanent members were added to the Security Council. The passage of a resolution now required 9 affirmative votes instead of 7. Since the enlargement of the Council was undertaken primarily for the benefit of the new nations, most of which were "neutralist" on East-West issues, it now became more difficult for the United States to control the Council. For example, in 1966, the United States attempted to have the Vietnam question inscribed on the Council's agenda, and found itself dependent upon the vote of Jordan. The move succeeded, but just barely. The days of an automatic American majority or of a "hidden veto," exercised by mobilizing this majority against a Soviet-sponsored resolution, were over. U.S. influence was still very great, but now had to depend on bargaining and persuasion rather than reliance on an absolute majority.

In considering the American position on the veto, one must also take notice of the considerable power the United States can exercise within UN organs before a vote is ever taken. At the present time, the United States pays approximately 40 percent of the total operating cost of the United Nations. It is largely this contribution that allows the Organization to maintain its present precarious hold on financial solvency. If the United States were to be sufficiently displeased with a project to consider withholding even just its voluntary contributions, UN planners would debate seriously before going ahead. On occasion, the United States has actually exercised this "financial veto" in order to attain objectives, such as the termination of the International Refugee Organization and the prevention of SUNFED, the Special United Nations Fund for Economic Development. In addition, the threat of a veto has at times been as effective as the actual casting of one. When, in 1950, the United States let it be known that it was determined to veto any candidate but Trygve Lie for the office of Secretary-General, the threat itself was sufficient. His term was extended by the General Assembly after the USSR had cast a veto in the Security Council.

In sum, the evidence demonstrates that the United States, like the Soviet Union, seeks to protect its national interest against any hostile action by the Security Council. However, because of its powerful position on the Security Council and in the United Nations generally, it has never been forced to resort to the casting of a veto. On the whole, therefore, the two superpowers have employed different parliamentary strategies to attain similar ends: the protection of the national interest.

The Veto and the United Nations

It now remains to be seen what effect the interaction of the two superpowers on the veto problem has had on the political evolution of the United Nations itself.

It is clear from the above discussion that the actual exercise of the veto power has not proved to be as great a threat to the effective functioning of the United Nations as it might have been in theory. In the first place, the Security Council has tended to narrow rather than expand the scope of the veto power. It established the principle that the abstention of a Great Power was not tantamount to a veto, thus giving states the opportunity to avoid commitment on a difficult choice without preventing UN action. In the Korean police-action decision of 1950, the Security Council went even further, by declaring that the absence of a Great Power should merely be regarded as an abstention, not a veto *in absentia*. Finally, the threat of the "double veto," the parliamentary device that would allow a Great Power to veto practically anything it chose, has not materialized in practice. While it still exists as a potential weapon, the "double veto" was used only three times, the last occasion arising in 1948.

Second, to blame the veto power for the strains and difficulties in resolving international problems is to confuse the symptoms with the causes. The Security Council veto might be viewed simply as the formal parliamentary expression of the real "veto" which any superpower actually has as a fact of life in a system of sovereign nation-states. The temptation of a voting assembly is to mistake its majority decisions as accurate and enforceable expressions of power realities. They are not, especially not in the nuclear age. The veto power has forced the Security Council to de-emphasize majority rule as far as the superpowers are concerned in favor of the more realistic unanimity principle: slow and frequently laborious negotiations to accommodate divergent points of view until both superpowers prefer to acquiesce rather than upset the system. The veto is thus a lesson in *Realpolitik*.

In fact, one may argue that the abolition of the veto might increase, not diminish, international tensions and the danger of war, since the majority might then be tempted to vote an action against a recalcitrant superpower. The technique of arriving at political decisions by counting votes without regard for power is a democratic luxury that the world may not be able to afford, particularly in the nuclear age. The principle of voting and living by majority decisions does make sense in a homogeneous political context, but in a world of profound schisms, negotiating with the opponent rather than outvoting him may be the wiser method of settling differences.

The third, and perhaps most important, effect of the veto has been its impact on the UN's political evolution. One reason why the veto has been less important in fact than it might have been in theory has been that other UN organs have taken up the slack created by a stymied Security Council. It is possible to chart three shifts in the locus of power among the organs of the United Nations, all of them due at least in part to the veto. First, by 1950, owing to the threat of the Soviet veto, the "Uniting for Peace" procedure brought an increasing number of peace and security issues before the General Assembly. The frequency of Security Council sessions in the early 1950's declined sharply and the scope of political issues that came before it narrowed considerably. In 1948, for example, the Council held 168 meetings, whereas in 1955, it held only 23. The Uniting for Peace Resolution—passed under strong American pressure and over vehement Soviet opposition—circumvented the paralysis of the Council and broadened the competence of the Assembly.

The Assembly, having had its own mandate enlarged in 1950, began to widen that of the Secretary-General by 1955. As we shall see in subsequent chapters, the missions of Dag Hammarskjöld to

Peking in 1955, to Suez in 1956, to Lebanon in 1958, and to the Congo in 1960 and 1961 were all based on Assembly resolutions which gave the Secretary-General increasing powers to make and execute policy. Indeed, the abortive Soviet attempt to replace the Office of the Secretary-General with a veto-bound triumvirate was in essence an effort to extend the principle of the veto into a new power center: the UN Secretariat.

Beginning in 1960, however, one could observe an interesting resuscitation of the Security Council, which was based on a more circumspect use of the Soviet veto. From the experience of the preceding years, the USSR knew that if it wielded a veto on a vital matter, the Assembly and the Secretary-General were liable to step into the breach and run the operation regardless. Hence, it began to abstain on issues which it might have vetoed before, preferring to keep even an undesirable operation in the Council, where it could exercise more influence than it could if the Assembly and the Secretary-General were in control. For example, at several points during the Congo Operation, the Soviet Union abstained on resolutions to which it was doubtless opposed. "Thus, Russia might well have vetoed the Council's resolution of 21 February 1961 which strengthened the hand of a Secretary-General whom the Russians had just branded as a 'criminal.' "[10] Abstention, the Soviets reasoned, might be the better part of wisdom.

The paradoxical result of this development is that the Council has been revived by—of all things—the Assembly. As one observer put it: "The 'Uniting for Peace' procedure may have seemed to rust, almost unused; but rust or not, the weapon hangs over the heads of the veto-wielding Council members. Each of these, a latter-day Damocles, is now inclined, when on the point of vetoing a resolution that might bring it down upon him, to swivel a wary eye at the ceiling and think again."[11] Between 1946 and 1959, the Soviet Union cast 88 vetoes or approximately 6.3 per year; from 1960 through 1968, it cast 17 or 1.2 per year, less than one-third as many.

In conclusion, then, the overall record suggests that there is less difference between the behavior of the superpowers in the United Nations than the 105-to-o vote score of the USSR and United

States would suggest. The United States developed over the years an effective "hidden veto" to protect its vital national interests, while many of the Soviet vetoes, particularly in areas not directly related to its national interest, were circumvented. In addition, the interaction of the superpowers over the veto question has led the United Nations away from the concept of majoritarianism to the more realistic principle of diplomacy in the settlement of major international disputes. Most important, however, is the fact that the circumvention of the Soviet vetoes has made the UN members use their organization in a flexible and imaginative manner. The Assembly, far from being a debating society, has exercised at times an important and significant role in several peace-keeping operations. The Secretary-General has been an active and important figure in the solution of international disputes, no lofty figurehead "above" politics. The United Nations has been actively engaged in solving political problems in a basically political manner—negotiation, pressure, compromise, and agreement.

The veto, then, has not been an insurmountable obstacle, but a constant incentive toward greater inventiveness and improvisation in international problem-solving. Perhaps more than any other single provision in the Charter, the veto has been responsible for the Charter's having remained a living document and the United Nations itself a living organization. It is true that the veto could have killed the United Nations. Thus far, the evidence suggests that it has made it stronger.

SELECTED BIBLIOGRAPHY

Bailey, Sydney D. "Veto in the Security Council," *International Conciliation*. No. 566 (January 1968).

Claude, Inis L., Jr. *Power and International Relations*. New York: Random House, 1962.

Jiménez de Arechaga, Eduardo. *Voting and the Handling of Disputes in the Security Council*. New York: Carnegie Endowment for International Peace, 1950.

Lee, Dwight E. "The Genesis of the Veto," *International Organization* (February 1947), pp. 33-42.

Moldaver, Arlette. "Repertoire of the Veto in the Security Council, 1946-1956," *International Organization* (Spring 1957), pp. 261-274.

Padelford, Norman J. "The Use of the Veto," *International Organization* (June 1948), pp. 227-246.

The Problem of the Veto in the United Nations Security Council, Staff Study No. 1, Subcommittee on the United Nations Charter, Committee on Foreign Relations, U.S. Senate, 83rd Congress, 2nd Session. Washington, D.C.: Government Printing Office, 1954.

CHAPTER 2

———•◆•———

The General Assembly:
The Problem of Membership
and the China Puzzle

Were Communist China also to become a permanent, veto-wielding member of the Security Council, that would, I fear, implant in the United Nations the seeds of destruction.

> John Foster Dulles
> U.S. Secretary of State
> June 28, 1957.

Those who speak out against the presence of the People's Republic of China within the United Nations have missed the bus of history.

> Valerian Zorin
> Soviet Delegate to the
> UN General Assembly
> October 22, 1962.

The Superpowers
and United Nations Membership Policy

The superpowers have had a decisive influence on the membership policy of the United Nations. One major criterion for admission stipulated in the Charter—that a state be "peace-loving"—has often been ignored in practice. In the overwhelming number of cases, little or no attention has been paid to the Advisory Opinion of the World Court in 1948, which stated that "every application for admission should be examined and voted on separately and on its own merits."[1] Instead, if one is to understand why only nine admissions marked the first decade of the UN's existence whereas over sixty new members joined the Organization during the second, one must examine the national policies of the superpowers. In UN admissions the change from competitive exclusion to accelerated entry policy was a result of superpower interaction.

During the first decade of the Organization's history, the policy of each superpower was to prevent the admission of the "friends" of the other. As noted in the preceding chapter, the United States accomplished this goal during the early years by the "hidden-veto" technique, while the Soviet Union made frequent use of the veto power against pro-Western states. Each superpower at times proposed "package deals" which the other rejected. The United States proposed the first such deal in 1946, but it was turned down by the Soviet Union. A year later, the positions were reversed when the United States rejected a Soviet "package" proposal. During the next eight years, the United States rejected several Soviet "packages," declaring its opposition to "horse trading" of this kind in principle and citing the 1948 World Court Advisory Opinion in support of its position. The United States abandoned this posture in 1955 when the superpowers agreed on a large "package" of sixteen new members: four Soviet-bloc nations—Albania, Bulgaria, Hungary, and Rumania; four Western nations—Ireland, Italy, Portugal, and Spain; and eight uncommitted nations—Austria, Cambodia, Ceylon, Finland, Jordan, Laos, Libya, and Nepal. This 1955 agreement ended the period of competitive exclusion in UN membership and ushered in a decade of rapid expansion.

The large majority of new members came from the emerging nations of Africa. The United States and the Soviet Union, in a complete reversal of form, now competed in welcoming gestures where they had previously competed in keeping the gates closed. By 1969, the only states still excluded against their own wishes were the partitioned countries—Germany, Vietnam, and Korea— and, of course, Communist China. In 1954, the membership of the United Nations had totaled sixty. By 1969, the total had more than doubled. A closer look at the radical difference in UN membership policy during the two decades reveals the decisive impact of the superpowers.

During the decade of competitive exclusion, 1946-1955, the United States adhered to a limited conception of its national interest. By rejecting "package" deals, it thwarted the ambitions of both pro-Western and neutral candidates for admission in order to exclude half a dozen Communist applicants. As a result, however, the original character and composition of the United Nations was largely preserved until 1955. This original membership included some Communist nations, but the overwhelming majority of states were pro-Western and accepted the leadership of the United States. In short, one result of the competitive exclusion policy was to perpetuate a United Nations in which the United States had virtually complete control, save for the Soviet veto power. The United States could not only obtain an automatic majority in the General Assembly, but could also produce the two-thirds majority that was necessary to approve Assembly action on important matters. It was this Assembly that directed most of the Korean "police-action." It was to this kind of Assembly that the United States was willing to bring future peace-keeping operations under the Uniting for Peace Resolution. And it was such an Assembly that often accepted the American lead on other vital East-West questions. The passage of the Uniting for Peace Resolution in 1950 over strenuous Soviet opposition—with 52 states supporting the American position, 5 against, and 2 abstentions—was a fair example of the U.S. dominance that characterized the decade of exclusion in membership policy.

The Soviet Union recognized, of course, that almost any kind of "package" deal was bound to improve its position within the Organization. Even a straight swap, one Communist state for one pro-Western, would strengthen the relative voting power on its side. It was also clear that an Assembly dominated by neutrals was less repugnant to the USSR than the existing one controlled by the United States and its allies. Thus, throughout the first decade, the Soviet Union sought "package" deals that would gain admission for its protégés, but was more willing than the United States to accept members of the opposite camp and neutral states in order to obtain the deal.

It is conceivable that if the period of competitive exclusion had lasted much longer, the potential of the United Nations might have been seriously stunted. Until the membership was broadened, the Organization had no claim to universality and thus only a limited right to speak as a voice of the world community. Moreover, in time the Soviet Union might have chosen to resign from this predominantly Western club in which it was condemned to the status of a permanent minority. Thus, if the policy of competitive exclusion had continued, the United States would have retained its absolute control, but over a decreasingly effective and influential organization. With the inception of a less restrictive membership policy, the United States had to settle for a less prominent role, but in a more broadly based and representative organization.

The year 1955 signaled the end of American hegemony over the General Assembly. The United States lost its automatic two-thirds majority, although it could still command a simple majority without much difficulty. During the next decade, when the birth of a new nation became almost a monthly event, the competition between the superpowers on the membership question produced virtually the opposite result from the exclusion of the previous ten years. The superpowers now competed in welcoming the new states. The number of states permitted to join during the second decade exceeded that of the original Charter members in 1945. Some of the new African states were accorded full UN privileges before they had actually cut their teeth as national states. The superpowers acted as if the new states were ready to run internationally before they had taken more than a few steps nationally.

The logic behind the new superpower policy was obvious. Outside the United Nations, it was becoming increasingly clear that the growing number of neutralist states would play an important role in the East-West struggle and both superpowers recognized UN membership as a good way to court new members. Within the United Nations, the Soviet Union had to win the support of the neutralists if it was ever to escape from its position of being a permanent minority, and the United States needed the support, or at least the benevolent neutrality, of the new nations if it was to retain its position of leadership. In the mid-1960's, the decade of rapid expansion came to an end. It ended for the simple reason that only a few states that wished to join the United Nations remained outside the system and only a handful of dependent territories had yet to become states.

The question "How did the superpowers' relative voting strengths change in the General Assembly during the decade of rapid expansion?" may best be answered by looking at some important votes in the 1960's. Votes on East-West issues could be grouped into five rough categories. First, there were those on which the United States remained clearly in control and only the Soviet bloc was in the opposition. A resolution passed in 1962 to continue the efforts of the UN Commission for the Unification and Rehabilitation of Korea (UNCURK) was a case in point. The vote was 63 in favor, 11 opposed, with 26 abstentions. Second, on some issues the United States managed to control a sizable majority, but had to lobby intensively to attain it. Thus, in 1960, it managed to persuade most Latin-American, Western European, and French-speaking African states to vote for Kasavubu rather than Lumumba to represent the government of the Congo. The vote was 53 in favor, 24 opposed, and 19 abstentions.

Third, there are times when the United States has to muster a "blocking third" in the General Assembly in order to defeat a Soviet initiative. Such was the case in 1967 when the Assembly met in emergency session to consider the aftermath of the Arab-Israeli war. The USSR, invoking a variant of the Uniting for Peace Resolution, had convened the session in the hope of persuading the General Assembly to brand Israel as an aggressor and to demand her unconditional withdrawal. The United States, on the other hand, supported the view that an Israeli withdrawal should be linked to recognition of the Jewish state. Neither the Soviet Union nor the United States was able to muster a two-thirds majority for its respective position. The draft resolution supported by the USSR failed to pass by a vote of 53 in favor, 46 opposed, with 20 abstentions; the U.S.-backed resolution suffered the same fate by a vote of 57 in favor, 43 opposed, with 20 abstentions. Each superpower had thus "neutralized" the other.

Fourth, on some issues, the United States came close to being defeated. The case par excellence is that of Chinese representation, which has come before every General Assembly since 1951 and which will be considered below.

More recently, yet another pattern has begun to emerge: U.S.-Soviet partnership on certain specific issues. For example, in 1968 the two superpowers submitted identical draft proposals for a nuclear nonproliferation treaty. The General Assembly endorsed this superpower initiative in June 1968 by a vote of 95 in favor, 4 against, with 21 abstentions.

Although it is true that the United States now had to work harder for its majorities than before, it retained two advantages over the Soviet Union in this struggle. First, since the United States was a leading military power and the leading financial contributor to the world organization, the American position was almost always given a respectful hearing in the Assembly. Second, the tradition of the United States in the intricacies of political lobbying, compromise, and majority rule may have given it an advantage over the other superpower, which was relatively unfamiliar with these concepts.

The issue of Chinese representation is an illuminating case study of superpower interaction in the General Assembly. The battle has been fought out between the United States and the Soviet Union against the background of the changing membership policy in the Assembly described above. Both superpowers mustered powerful resources in support of their opposing positions and both attempted to adapt their tactics to a constantly changing membership.

The Superpowers
and the Struggle over Chinese Representation

The problem of Chinese representation first arose in 1949 as a result of the Communist conquest of mainland China. But since the Communists had not destroyed the Nationalist regime, which had entrenched itself in Formosa, there were now two governments, each of which claimed the Chinese seat in the United Nations. In November 1949, the Communist People's Republic of China (CPR) cabled the President of the General Assembly, challenging the legal status of the Nationalist delegation and claiming that it did not speak for the Chinese people. This was followed in January 1950 by similar cables to the Security Council.[2] The Soviet Union immediately supported the Chinese Communist claims, and when the Security Council, upon strong American urging, refused to recognize them, the Soviet representative walked out in protest. Since that time, the United States has staked its political prestige on keeping Communist China out, and the Soviet Union, while at times showing somewhat ambiguous behavior, has always voted for the entry of Red China.

At the time of the initial claim of the CPR, 46 nations recognized the Nationalist regime, while only 16, including the United Kingdom and India, recognized the new Communist government. The simultaneous existence of two governments, each claiming to represent the same state, brought up the problem of the relationship between national recognition and UN representation. Secretary-General Trygve Lie addressed himself to this issue in a legal memorandum on March 8, 1950.

The Secretary-General declared that it was "unfortunate" that "the question of representation had been linked up with the question of recognition." These were legally separable issues. Indeed, a state might recognize one regime as the government of a member state and another as the government qualified to represent that state in the United Nations. He pointed out the unique character of the China problem, since for the first time in the history of the United Nations two rival governments were claiming the same seat. He then implied that the CPR was better qualified to occupy the Chinese seat:

> It is submitted that the proper principles can be derived by analogy from Article 4 of the Charter. This Article requires that an applicant for membership must be able and willing to carry out the obligations of membership. The obligations of membership can be carried out only by governments which in fact possess the power to do so. Where a revolutionary government presents itself as representing a state, in rivalry to an existing government, the question at issue should be which of these two governments in fact is in a position to employ the resources and direct the people of the state in fulfillment of the obligations of membership. In essence this means an inquiry as to whether the new government exercises effective authority within the territory of the state and is habitually obeyed by the bulk of the population.
>
> If so, it would seem to be appropriate for the United Nations organs, through their collective action, to accord it the right to represent the state in the Organization, even though

individual Members of the Organization refuse, and may continue to refuse, to accord it recognition as the lawful government for reasons which are valid under their national policies.[3]

Mr. Lie's initiative evoked powerful U.S. resistance and provided one of the sparks that ignited the American attack on the Secretariat discussed in the following chapter. The Soviet Union supported the Secretary-General's position, while the United States disputed it in a legal memorandum of its own:

A revolutionary government to be recognized for purposes of representation must exercise effective authority, be based on the consent of the population, be able and willing to achieve the purposes of the Charter and fulfill its obligations under the Charter and international law, and respect human rights and fundamental freedoms.[4]

The Lie memorandum and the American response to it marked the beginning of the confusion which has surrounded the China issue ever since. First, Lie's major criterion of "effective authority" was primarily a *de facto* political argument. The American rebuttal emphasized the moral qualifications of the government to be represented. Thus, as Inis L. Claude has pointed out, "the treatment of the membership question as a political and moral problem leads ultimately to the *confusion* of the issue."[5] Second, Lie's position did not make clear what would happen to the Nationalist government if the CPR were seated. Moreover, by invoking Article 4 of the Charter, which deals with the admission of members, the Secretary-General left himself open to the argument that he was confusing a problem of representation with one of admission. Finally, several nations, notably the United Kingdom, were placed in the anomalous position of recognizing the CPR on their own, but dealing with the Nationalist government in the United Nations.

Strong American pressure prevented a vote on Mr. Lie's proposal. Instead, the entire debate on the Chinese representation question was transferred to the General Assembly when that body, on December 14, 1950, recommended that "whenever more than one authority claims to be the government entitled to represent a member state," the question should be considered "in the light of the Purposes and Principles of the Charter and the circumstances of each case," and that "the attitude adopted by the General Assembly should be taken into account in other organs of the United Nations and in the specialized agencies."[6] This resolution, while implying that the Assembly be a guide for other UN organs, also implied that each of the major UN organs should have the right, under its own rules of procedure, to decide on questions of representation. Hence, the state of China might be represented by the Nationalist government in one part of the United Nations, but by the CPR in another.

This issue between the superpowers was now squarely joined. After boycotting the Council for a brief period, the Soviet Union returned in August 1950 to demand that the CPR be seated promptly in all organs of the United Nations as the legitimate government of China and that the Nationalist government be ousted. The entire Soviet bloc, of course, supported this position, and a small number of other states also favored the seating of the CPR without, however, proposing the simultaneous ousting of the Chiang Kai-shek regime. Precisely how they would deal with the Nationalist government was not made clear. This coalition marshalled a number of arguments in favor of CPR representation in 1950. It was held that the United Nations would be more effective if it were universal, and that events had shown that the CPR was in *de facto* control of continental China. Some states also felt that Communist China might be checked more effectively inside the United Nations than out, especially on matters of disarmament and arms control. The presence of other potentially aggressive states in the United Nations had, in any case, diluted the "peace-loving" provision in the Charter. Finally, it was argued that the Chinese "veto" would not add power to that of the USSR, which alone was sufficient to block Security Council action.

The opposing camp was led by the United States, which based its objections on the grounds that the CPR was an illegal, immoral, as well as a nonpermanent, government. The CPR's intervention in the Korean War and the General Assembly's finding of aggression underlined the "nonpeace-loving" character of the regime. To seat it would imply a condonement of aggression, according to this view, that might inspire other potential aggressors to try to "shoot their way" into the United Nations. In 1954, the United States, in its eagerness to keep the CPR out, asserted through Secretary of State John Foster Dulles that the veto power governing the admission of new members was also applicable, by necessary and unchallengeable analogy, to the issue of Chinese representation.[7] Indeed, the Secretary of State went so far as to suggest that the veto could be eliminated on questions of admission but retained on matters of representation.[8]

From 1951 to 1960, the issue of Chinese representation came before every session of the General Assembly under the so-called "moratorium device." Under this technique, the United States proposed each year that consideration of the question be deferred. This position was adopted by the Assembly at every session until 1960. The voting figures are shown on p. 31.[9]

The impact of changing UN membership policy may be seen clearly in the voting record on the China question. The absolute number of votes in favor of the moratorium remained fairly constant during the ten years, but since during this same period the membership of the United Nations grew by 65 percent, the relative percentage of states supporting the American position declined significantly. The U.S. position suffered its major losses in 1956 and 1960; 1956 was the first year in which the members admitted through the 1955 "package deal" voted on the issue. As a result, percentage support of the U.S. position dropped ten points and the direct opposition to the American position doubled in strength. The second major drop occurred in 1960, when seventeen new members joined the organization. Now the American position was in serious jeopardy, for the supporters of the moratorium won by only a plurality and the combined votes of the opposition, abstainers, and absentees exceeded the U.S. position by fifteen votes.

Hence, the change in UN membership policy was one factor that forced the United States to adopt new parliamentary tactics on the China question in 1961. In addition, it had become clear to many that the Communist regime was more than just a passing phase and was therefore entitled to membership. Many of the newly admitted states, which wanted expansion of the Security Council and of the Economic and Social Council, were aware that the Soviet Union would not permit revision of the Charter unless

VOTING PATTERNS ON CHINESE REPRESENTATION
UNDER THE "MORATORIUM DEVICE," 1951–1960

Session	For	Against	Abstaining	Absent	Total	Percent Supporting the U.S. Position
6th (1951)	37	11	4	8	60	61
7th (1952)	42	7	11	0	60	70
8th (1953)	44	10	2	4	60	73
9th (1954)	43	11	6	0	60	72
10th (1955)	42	12	6	0	60	70
11th (1956)	47	24	8	0	79	60
12th (1957)	48	27	7	0	82	59
13th (1958)	44	28	9	0	81	54
14th (1959)	44	29	9	0	82	54
15th (1960)	42	34	22	1	99	42

the CPR was admitted to its "rightful" seat in the United Nations. Finally, an increasing number of members felt that the United Nations could hardly expect Red China to observe the UN Charter if at the same time the United Nations denied that nation membership status and the right to participate in UN proceedings.

On the other hand, quite apart from continued American pressure, the opposition to seating the CPR was still formidable. The CPR's position that it would accept nothing less than the expulsion of the "Taiwan clique" ruled out a "two-Chinas" solution that many members looked upon with favor. Moreover, if Peking was serious about the "restoration of China's legitimate rights" in Formosa and proceeded to "liberate" that island, then seating the CPR, in the opinion of many, would mean that "the UN should acquiesce in Communist China's design to conquer Taiwan and the 11 million people who live there and thereby to overthrow and abolish the independent government of the Republic of China."[10]

The Sixteenth General Assembly in 1961 marked the beginning of a new phase in the evolution of the Chinese representation issue. Not only had the membership of the Assembly changed, but momentous developments had taken place between the two Communist giants. Great fissures had begun to appear in the Moscow-Peking Alliance and an ideological controversy of the first magnitude was well under way. Yet, the USSR, in its public pronouncements, continued its ten-year-old agitation on behalf of Communist China.

The United States, in turn, had concluded that there was no hope of warding off a full-scale debate on the China issue. Therefore, it altered its tactics and instead of trying to prevent debate, sought to have the issue debated in as favorable a form and climate as possible. First, the United States made a major move to obtain support for its position by agreeing to permit the simultaneous admission of Mongolia and Mauritania to UN membership. This, it was hoped, would help to win the good will of many African states on the China issue. Second, the United States was aware that a direct vote on a resolution to seat the CPR and eject the Nationalists was technically a matter of credentials, thus requiring only a simple majority vote. Hence, the American plan was to forestall such a vote by entering a draft resolution asking the Assembly to declare in advance that the China problem was "an important question," and therefore, in accordance with Article 18 of the Charter, one requiring a two-thirds majority.

The actual debate on the China question occupied twelve plenary sessions of the Assembly. During the debate, the major obstacle preventing a compromise was the attitude of the two Chinas themselves. The only thing that the Nationalists and the CPR were in agreement on was that neither would sit in the United Nations if the other China were also seated. The superpowers held to their opposing positions.

When the American-sponsored draft resolution declaring the Chinese representation issue an "important question" came to a vote on December 15, 1961, it was adopted by a vote of 61 to 34, with 7 abstentions and 3 absences. The Soviet proposal requiring the immediate seating of the CPR and the simultaneous ousting of the Chiang regime did not even get a simple majority. It was defeated by a vote of 37 to 48, with 19 abstentions. A three-power (Cambodia, Ceylon, and Indonesia) amendment to the Soviet draft resolution, which would have provided for the seating of the CPR but did not propose the expulsion of the Nationalists, was also rejected by a vote of 30 in favor, 45 against, and 29 abstentions. Thus, the United States, by a judicious change in tactics, more than held the line in 1961.

When the Chinese question arose again at the Seventeenth General Assembly in October 1962, China had just launched her border attack on India in the Himalayas. This development undoubtedly heightened doubts about the willingness of the CPR to accept the obligations of the Charter. India, however, continued to advocate the seating of Red China, arguing that the "only way to check Chinese military adventurism was to make it accept its responsibilities as a member of the Organization and thereby be subject to the views and discipline of the General Assembly."[11]

The Soviet Union, despite the worsening of Sino-Soviet relations, attacked the "two-Chinas" solution and declared that "those who speak out against the presence of the People's Republic of China within the United Nations have missed the bus of history."[12] The United States stood fast.

When the vote was taken on October 30, it appeared that it was the Communists who had missed the bus. The Soviet resolution to eject Chiang's representatives and seat the CPR was rejected by a vote of 42 to 56, with 12 abstentions. This vote indicated a definite shift against the CPR: the absolute number of votes against the CPR increased by 8, while those in favor increased by only 5. The 8 new votes against the CPR were cast by African nations which had abstained the previous year: Central African Republic, Chad, Congo (Brazzaville), Congo (Leopold-ville), Dahomey, Ivory Coast, Niger, and Upper Volta. A spokesman for this group noted that these states still foresaw the eventual seating of Red China, but that they did not favor the exclusion of Nationalist China. He also questioned Peking's peaceful intentions in the light of the attack on India.[13] All in all, the year 1962 showed a significant reversal of the pro-CPR trend and much of the membership favoring a compromise solution. But those favoring a compromise were now closer to the American than to the Soviet position. In 1963, the voting pattern remained almost the same. An Albanian-sponsored draft resolution to oust Chiang and seat the CPR was defeated by a vote of 41 to 57, with 12 abstentions.

No vote was taken in 1964. In 1965, an American-sponsored draft resolution declaring the Chinese representation issue an "important question" was adopted by a vote of 56 to 49, with 11 abstentions, and an Albanian proposal to seat the CPR and oust the Nationalist regime was defeated by a vote of 47 to 47, with 20 abstentions. Even though the former vote was decisive, since it ruled out the seating of the CPR by a simple majority, the United States was disturbed by the closeness of the vote on the issue itself. In 1966, however, the excesses of the "Cultural Revolution" had alienated some of the Afro-Asian nations, and the U.S. position gained once again. This time the vote making China an "important question" was 66 to 48, with 7 abstentions, and an Albanian proposal identical to the one advanced the previous year was defeated by a vote of 56 to 46, with 17 abstentions. An Italian-sponsored proposal to appoint a special committee to investigate the CPR's position vis-à-vis UN membership and to report to the Assembly by July 1967 was also defeated by a vote of 62 to 34, with 25 abstentions. The patterns for 1967 and 1968 showed little change. In 1967, the votes on the three different aspects of the problem were 69-48-4, 58-45-17, and 57-32-30, respectively. In 1968, they were 73-47-51, 58-44-23, and 67-30-27.

Thus, by the late 1960's, the American effort to exclude Communist China was still successful. Many observers, however, attributed this development less to American persuasive power than to the policies of mainland China itself.

Conclusions

There can be little doubt that the China question has been one of the most important testing grounds of the strength and influence of the superpowers in the General Assembly. Both took opposing positions from the beginning and held to them throughout the long struggle. Yet, during the course of the struggle, the Assembly itself underwent significant changes.

The record shows a gradual erosion of the American position during the 1950's. But this erosion was not accompanied by a comparable burst of support for the Soviet position. Rather, most of the new states favored a compromise solution which was acceptable to neither of the superpowers nor to the two Chinese regimes themselves. When, in 1961, the United States was forced to give up the moratorium device and to face the issue squarely, it was able to persuade the General Assembly to treat the China problem as an "important question." It has been able to do so every year since then. Actually, as it turned out, the USSR was unable to obtain even a simple majority on its proposal to seat the CPR and expel the Nationalists. In 1962, the Chinese attack on India took its toll in the Assembly and resulted in a reversal of the pro-CPR trend which seemed to have been established during the 1950's.

When Albania replaced the Soviet Union as the main sponsor of pro-CPR resolutions in 1963, the CPR fared no better. Only in 1965 did the CPR come close to winning. The years 1966, 1967, and 1968 again saw a sharp decline in pro-CPR strength.

The most important factor in the equation has been the growth in membership. Most of the new states have not regarded the

China problem as of paramount importance to their interests, but have been quite sensitive to the fact that the issue has been vital to the two superpowers. On the whole, the United States has influenced the uncommitted nations more effectively than has the Soviet Union, probably because it has maneuvered more adroitly and has been better grounded in the tactics of parliamentary politics. When the United States realized that a substantive discussion could no longer be postponed, it did not fight a losing battle for another moratorium, but waged a successful fight on the issue itself. U.S. negotiators also let it be known that the seating of Red China would be unpopular with the U.S. Congress and might have adverse effects on American financial support of the United Nations. The Soviet Union, by insisting on the expulsion of the Nationalists, robbed itself of the support of many uncommitted countries that favored the seating of the CPR, but not the concomitant exclusion of "the other China."

If the Chinese case illustrates anything about the role of the superpowers in the General Assembly, it shows that the large Afro-Asian influx has not brought about an automatic reduction in American power. To be sure, this power no longer produces easy majorities, as in the early years, but if used with adroitness and a sense of proportion, it is still very much intact. And while the Soviet-bloc membership in the United Nations has doubled, the actual impact of the USSR on the Assembly has not risen significantly, if at all. In terms of sheer numbers, the Afro-Asian nations have, of course, enjoyed a tremendous rise in voting power. But when their vital interests are not at stake, as in the China issue, they still permit the superpowers to lead. And in this struggle for leadership, the United States has proved itself to be somewhat more successful than its antagonist.

SELECTED BIBLIOGRAPHY

Alker, Hayward R., Jr., and Bruce M. Russett. *World Politics in the General Assembly*. New Haven: Yale University Press, 1965.
Bailey, Sydney D. *The General Assembly of the United Nations*. New York: Praeger, 1960.

The Problem of Membership in the United Nations, Staff Study No. 3,
    Subcommittee on the United Nations Charter, Committee on For-
    eign Relations, U.S. Senate, 83rd Congress, 2nd Session. Washing-
    ton, D.C.: Government Printing Office, 1954.

Rudzinski, Aleksander W. "Admission of New Members: The United
    Nations and the League of Nations," *International Conciliation,* No.
    480 (April 1952).

Steiner, H. Arthur. "Communist China in the World Community," *Inter-
    national Conciliation,* No. 533 (May 1961).

The Secretary-General: The American and Soviet Attacks on the Secretariat, 1952 and 1960

Startling evidence has disclosed infiltration into the United Nations of an overwhelmingly large group of disloyal United States citizens, many of whom are clearly associated with the international Communist movement.

> Presentment of U.S. Federal
> Grand Jury, December 1952.

Everyone has heard how vigorously the imperialist countries defend the attitude of Mr. Hammarskjöld. Is it not clear whose interests he interprets and executes, whose "saint" he is?

> Premier Nikita Khrushchev
> UN General Assembly
> October 3, 1960.

"It may be true," said Dag Hammarskjöld shortly before he died, "that in a very deep, human sense there is no neutral individual, because everyone, if he is worth anything, has to have his ideas and ideals. . . . But what I do claim is that even a man who is in that sense not neutral can very well undertake and carry through neutral actions because that is an act of integrity."[1] This statement, which was made in response to Premier Khrushchev's blunt assertion that no man could be neutral, probably best expresses the philosophical conception of the UN Secretary-Generalship.

One of the greatest fears of the founders of the United Nations was that the new world organization would be no more than the sum of its parts—a group of delegates each loyal to his own nation and perceiving the world through the particular lenses of his own nationality. The men at San Francisco were deeply convinced that one important road to international order could be constructed by providing the United Nations with a nucleus of men and women who, for the duration of their tenure as world civil servants, would be loyal to the world community and not seek or receive instructions from any national government. It was this notion of international loyalty-building that provided the rationale for the Office of the Secretary-General and of his staff, the UN Secretariat.

The Office of the Secretary-General of the United Nations is not without precedent. The League of Nations had made provision for such a post. Its first incumbent, Sir Eric Drummond, a British civil servant, was primarily an administrator who made it his policy to remain aloof from the political disputes that were sapping the lifeblood of the League. Albert Thomas, on the other hand, the Director-General of the League's International Labor Organization, set quite another precedent. Not content with anonymous administrative responsibilities, he ventured into the uncharted lands of international statesmanship and took stands on controversial policy issues. Weighing these two precedents and seeing value in both, the UN architects endowed the Office of the United Nations Secretary-General with political as well as administrative powers. The Secretary-General was not only to be the chief administrative officer of the United Nations, but, in the words of the Preparatory Commission in 1945, his Office was to represent

> A quite special right which goes beyond any power previously accorded to the head of an international organization. The Secretary-General more than anyone else will stand for the United Nations as a whole. In the eyes of the world, no less than in the eyes of his own staff he must embody the ideals and principles of the Charter.[2]

This conception of the Office led to the inclusion in the Charter of Articles 98 and 99, which set forth the Secretary-General's significant political powers. Under Article 98, the Secretary-General may be entrusted with broad discretionary powers by the major organs of the Organization. And under Article 99, "the Secretary-General may bring to the attention of the Security Council any matter which in his opinion may threaten the maintenance of international peace and security." The founders of the United Nations thus clearly intended the Secretary-General to be an international statesman, a kind of conscience of the world. In order to equip him adequately for this role, they gave him what, in some respects at least, amounted to the power of acting as a twelfth member of the Security Council.

Each of the superpowers at different times was involved in a frontal attack against the Office of the Secretary-General. In 1952, rampant forces of anti-Communism in the United States aimed their attack on the authority of the Secretary-General as chief administrative officer of the Organization; in 1960, the Soviet Union attempted to paralyze the political initiative of the Secretary-General as international statesman with its "troika" proposal. The Secretariat and the Secretary-Generalship withstood both assaults, but not without major crises which shook the United Nations. A comparative analysis of these two events sheds important light on the U.S.–Soviet confrontation at the United Nations and its effects on the political evolution of the world organization.

The American Attack

The first Secretary-General of the United Nations was Trygve Lie of Norway. Lie used his political powers abundantly and took positions in conflicts among the major powers from the very start. In 1946, he submitted a memorandum on his own initiative regarding the power of the Security Council to retain on the agenda an item on Soviet troop withdrawals from Iran. Two years later, he supported the European Recovery Program and opted in favor of the partition of Palestine. Soon thereafter, he became embroiled in political controversies of the first magnitude. Early in 1950, Mr. Lie advocated the seating of the Chinese Communist delegation in the United Nations and provoked the extreme displeasure of the United States. Several weeks later, he strongly supported American initiative in the "police action" to repel aggression by

North Korea, and went so far as to label the North Koreans as the aggressors. While this action reconciled the United States, it provoked the implacable hostility of the Soviet Union. When, in late 1950, the question of Lie's reappointment came up, the United States threatened to veto the appointment of any other candidate, while the Soviet Union declared with equal conviction that it would not tolerate Lie. The United States prevailed upon the General Assembly to "extend" his term for another three years. Yet, ironically, it was not from the Soviet Union but from the United States that the major attack on the Secretariat came during Trygve Lie's extended term.

The U.S. attack on the Secretariat during 1952 and 1953 had its roots in the American political conditions at the time. Early in 1950, the trial of Alger Hiss had raised the specter of Communist infiltration in positions of high official responsibility. Shortly thereafter, Senator Joseph McCarthy launched an attack on the State Department, claiming that it was infested with Communists. Although a special Senate subcommittee, the Tydings Committee, called McCarthy's charge "a fraud and a hoax" as early as July 1950, a connection was made in the public mind between these charges and recent setbacks in U.S. foreign policy, as in China.

At the same time, the United States was undergoing a difficult period of readjustment in the United Nations. The early, if over-optimistic, hopes for global peace through the world organization had given way to the harsh realities of the cold war. The extensive use of the Soviet veto was resented by many Americans. The rising voices of colonial peoples put the United States into an embarrassing position between its revolutionary heritage of independence and its important NATO allies. Most important, the United States was bearing the brunt of a costly and bloody war in Korea and its protracted peace negotiations. These two trends—the fear of Communist infiltration, inspired by McCarthy, and disillusionment with the United Nations—were important ingredients in the American attack on the Secretariat.

During the summer of 1952, a Special Federal Grand Jury was impaneled in New York to investigate possible violations of U.S. laws by American citizens working in the UN Secretariat. The refusal of several staff members to answer questions about affiliations with the Communist Party attracted the attention of the American public and of Secretary-General Trygve Lie.[3] On October 13, 1952, the day before the opening of the Seventh General Assembly, the Internal Security Subcommittee of the Senate Judiciary Committee moved to New York and opened public hearings on the activities of U.S. citizens employed by the United Nations. During these Subcommittee sessions, held October 12–15, twenty-four current and four former employees of the United Nations testified. Of the twenty-four current employees, seventeen invoked the Fifth Amendment on questions related to past or present associations with the Communist Party.[4] Of the seven current employees who did not invoke the Fifth Amendment, three admitted past membership in the Communist Party and a fourth was implicated by the testimony of an outside witness.[5]

Immediately following this testimony, Secretary-General Lie took rapid steps to try to stem the rising tide of American criticism. Because of the varying tenures of the UN employees and their different behavior before the Senate Subcommittee, the Secretary-General was faced with three separate dilemmas. First, should he dismiss the three temporary American employees who admitted that they had once been Communists? Second, should he fire the seven temporary employees who had invoked the Fifth Amendment? And third, how should he deal with the ten permanent UN officials who had invoked their U.S. constitutional privilege of silence and who, as international civil servants, were protected by immunities?

Secretary-General Lie took a clear and immediate stand to discharge those temporary employees who admitted past Communist affiliations. First, he argued, an American Communist was not a representative American citizen, since the United States had declared the party subversive and dedicated to the forcible overthrow of its government. Second, because the UN Headquarters was in the United States, the Secretary-General felt that "it was plain common sense not to want any American Communists in the Secretariat."[6] He explained the presence of the few Communists by stating that haste in the hiring of personnel in 1946 had made adequate screening of applicants very difficult, and that his requests to the Department of State and FBI for information on

U.S. applicants at first had met with no response. When, in 1949, the State Department finally agreed to examine records of U.S. applicants for UN jobs, it still refused to provide the Secretary-General with adequate information upon which he could base an independent judgment. For example, not only had the evaluations been extremely slow in coming through, but they had usually been one-word summaries, such as "questionable" or "reject." The Secretary-General had not been willing to dismiss an employee on the basis of such limited material. Moreover, not until March 1, 1952, had the Secretary-General been empowered to dismiss temporary staff members without giving any other reason than that such action would be in the best interests of the Organization. Thus, he could not have dismissed UN employees on the basis of the U.S. reports even if he had wanted to.

The problem of temporary UN employees who refused to answer the Internal Security Subcommittee's questions was more complicated. Yet, the Secretary-General was of the opinion that these employees, too, should be dismissed. He defended his action as follows:

United Nations immunity extended only to acts of Secretariat members in their official capacity. It did not extend to their outside activities or private lives. I felt strongly that a United Nations official should cooperate fully with investigations conducted by an official agency of his own government, at least in those countries where Western democratic traditions protected him from the exercise of arbitrary power. . . . Furthermore, by virtue of the very fact that a United Nations official was an international civil servant, special obligations were imposed upon him to conduct himself vis-à-vis the Member governments at all times in a manner above just reproach. This latter opinion was fully shared by the General Assembly when it adopted Article 1.4 of the Staff Regulations, which read:

Members of the Secretariat shall conduct themselves at all times in a manner of conduct befitting their status as international civil servants. They shall not engage in any activity that is incompatible with the proper discharge of their duties with the United Nations. They shall avoid any action and in particular any kind of of public pronouncement which may adversely reflect on their status. While they are not expected to give up their national sentiments or their political and religious convictions, they shall at all times bear in mind the reserve and tact incumbent upon them by reason of their international status.

I believed that to plead a privilege against self-incrimination, though it was a constitutional right, would be clearly in violation of Article 1.4, except in extraordinary circumstances.[7]

Lie also felt that these UN officials had to be discharged because they "tended under the circumstances to discredit the Secretariat as a whole, to cast suspicion on all the staff—and, still more serious, imperil the position of the Organization in the host country."[8] He therefore dismissed those Americans with temporary contracts who had invoked the Fifth Amendment. In all cases of dismissal, however, the Secretary-General first ascertained to his own satisfaction that the employees had, in fact, been connected with subversive organizations at one time.

The heart of the controversy centered around the third group: the ten staff members with permanent contracts who had refused to answer certain questions. Lie immediately placed the involved personnel on compulsory leave while he considered his next move. To aid him in reaching a decision, the Secretary-General, on October 27, constituted a special three-man panel of eminent international jurists, consisting of Messrs. E. S. Herbert, W. D. Mitchell, and P. Veldekens. This body, on November 29, 1952, recommended "the dismissal from the United Nations staff of all active members of the U.S. Communist Party or other organizations officially declared subversive."[9] They further recommended that all UN employees of U.S. nationality who refused to answer questions about their past or present Communist Party membership should be dismissed because their action created a "suspicion of guilt." They claimed that such a refusal to answer questions was a fundamental breach of Article 1.4 of the Staff Regulations, and that the Secretary-General was therefore empowered to dismiss the ten staff members with permanent contracts who had refused to cooperate with the Senate Subcommittee. Finally, they advised the Secretary-General to be guided by the views of the host country in security matters.

Acting upon the advice of the jurists, Lie notified the employees that he would have to dismiss them if they did not state their intention to answer questions within three days. This they declined to do, and so, on December 4, they were formally discharged. Once again, however, Lie made a private investigation regarding each dismissal.

The discharge of the employees was ill-timed. Just two days before, on December 2, the Federal Grand Jury, which had held hearings throughout this period, made its public presentment. It declared that "startling evidence [had] disclosed infiltration into the United Nations of an overwhelmingly large group of disloyal United States citizens, many of whom [were] closely associated with the international Communist movement."[10] Previous criminal records and morals charges of American UN officials were also publicized. The Grand Jury presentment concluded by saying that it had found that "in some of the most flagrant and obvious cases of disloyalty, the State Department [had given] a clean bill of health."

Unfortunately, the dismissal of the Secretariat employees two days after the Grand Jury report seemed to confirm the presumption that the United Nations was indeed harboring subversives. Ironically, Lie's action had been based entirely upon the performance of the Secretariat employees at the Senate Subcommittee hearings, since no copy of the Grand Jury proceedings had been available. In addition, the Grand Jury presentment, while it leveled a general charge against the United Nations, did not return a single indictment. As Trygve Lie later noted: "Had there been any meaningful evidence of illegal subversive activity against any member of the Secretariat, it would have returned indictments in accordance with its duty. It did not return even one; but its 'presentment' made a blanket and indiscriminate finding of 'Guilty.' "[11]

Lie's troubles did not end with the dismissals; they had only begun. Sentiment throughout the United States was rising against the United Nations as well as the State Department, which allegedly had cleared some of the persons involved. On January 1, 1953, the State Department, perhaps in an effort to relieve the heat on itself, supplied the Internal Security Subcommittee with a list of thirty-eight UN Secretariat employees who had received "adverse comments" in their loyalty reports. At the time the list was released, twenty-seven of the thirty-eight were no longer employed by the United Nations.[12] On January 7, 1953, Senator Pat McCarran introduced a bill to prevent citizens of questionable loyalty from accepting employment in the United Nations and proposed a procedure whereby any American applying for a UN job would first have to be cleared by the FBI and other U.S. Security agencies. At one point, U.S. investigators actually moved into UN buildings to check existing UN employees of U.S. nationality. In psychological and symbolic terms, this was probably more damaging than the establishment of routine procedure for clearing new applicants for the staff. Lie, in an attempt to reassure the American public, stated in his report of January 30 that "the UN work[ed] in a glass house, not only physically, but in every respect. It [was] not a profitable place for spies and saboteurs. No military secrets [were] ever handled by the Secretariat."[13] Nevertheless, both the Grand Jury and two Senate subcommittees continued investigations of UN personnel in 1953.

In all, twenty temporary and permanent employees had been discharged from the UN Secretariat during 1952 for admitting past membership in the Communist Party or for invoking the Fifth Amendment. One additional staff member, who invoked the Fifth Amendment at hearings early in 1953, was also dismissed. These twenty-one employees brought their cases before the UN Administrative Tribunal, an impartial appeal board for aggrieved UN employees. On September 1, 1953, the Tribunal ruled that one of the ten temporary employees had been fired in breach of contract and that ten of the eleven permanent employees had been fired illegally. The Tribunal ordered reinstatement in four cases and compensation in lieu of reinstatement in the other seven.[14] Thus, the Secretary-General was faced with a new dilemma: how should he react to the decision of a UN Tribunal which had ruled against the obvious wishes of a superpower?

Lie decided not to reinstate any of the discharged Secretariat members. The Administrative Tribunal therefore reconsidered these four cases and, on October 13, 1953, fixed total compensation for the entire group of eleven. They were awarded full salary up to the date of the Tribunal's judgment plus $300 each for legal costs. Total compensation for the illegal firing was fixed at $170,730 plus pension rights in one case.[15] The United States bitterly contested this ruling and held that the General Assembly was not obligated to accept it. The Assembly, in turn, on December 9, referred the question to the International Court for an advisory opinion.[16]

On July 13, 1954, the International Court of Justice, in a 9-to-3 opinion, with the American justice in dissent, supported the ruling of the Administrative Tribunal.[17] Total compensation was eventually fixed at $179,420.[18] The U.S. Congress declared that no American funds paid to the United Nations could be used to pay compensation to the dismissed officials.[19] Thus, Lie faced yet another problem: how to pay the compensation costs? To cooperate with the American government in meeting the issue presented by Congress, the money was not paid out of the UN's regular budget, but out of the Tax Equalization Fund. Since this Fund was not supported by contributions from member states, but by the UN staff in order to equalize tax burdens, the device adopted met the Congressional stipulation.

One additional hurdle remained: the U.S. requirement that American citizens applying for positions with the United Nations be cleared first by the U.S. government. After the crisis had passed, an arrangement for security clearances was worked out between the American government and the United Nations. Under this agreement, each applicant must be processed by the U.S. security system. The American government reserved to itself the right to give information and advice to the Secretariat on the basis of its investigations, but not to dictate personnel policy. In practice, nevertheless, it did prove difficult, on at least one occasion, for the Secretary-General to decline the "advice" of Washington. In 1954, for example, Ambassador Henry Cabot Lodge sharply criticized the Director-General of UNESCO for not dismissing summarily all Americans on his staff who had received negative loyalty reports.[20] In recent years, there have been no major clashes over the issue, but it is nevertheless true that the U.S.

government wields significant potential power over UN personnel policy, which may border on an infringement of the Secretary-General's role as the UN's chief administrative officer.

The entire episode, if looked at in perspective, suggests several important conclusions. First, it is important to remember that the State Department and the Executive of the U.S. government did not launch the attack. It was precipitated by the extremists in the American public and by reactionary elements in the Congress. The Executive was caught in the middle between domestic pressures and international responsibilities. The pressure exerted on the Executive Branch made it necessary to urge the Secretary-General to give in to the demands.

Second, the Secretary-General largely complied with all the American demands, though not always in the summary fashion demanded of him. The crisis was composed of five separate parts: the discharge of temporary employees; the discharge of permanent employees; the decision of the Administrative Tribunal to reinstate four employees; the payment of compensation; and the security-clearance system. The United States had its way on each point, except the payment of compensation, although the United Nations did meet Congressional stipulations regarding the method of payment. Whatever the intrinsic merits of the case, the Secretary-General found it virtually impossible to resist the pressure of the American superpower. As one authority put it, "[The Secretary-General] believed that the Communist problem in the Secretariat was objectively a molehill, but recognized that it had become a subjective mountain which had to be removed if the United Nations was not to be destroyed by the withdrawal of American public support."[21]

Third, and perhaps most important, the Secretariat recovered its balance. It gave ground on certain important points during the crisis, but the fundamental principles of the international civil service and the independence of the Secretary-General were not destroyed. The Secretariat weathered the American attack in 1952 and 1953, just as it had endured the Soviet three-year boycott of Trygve Lie from 1950 to 1953 and would endure the Soviet assault to be analyzed below. But there was irony as well as pathos in the American attack, because at that time the Secretary-

General was already under heavy censure and even boycott by the Soviet bloc. As Trygve Lie poignantly wrote, looking back on the period:

> Their [the Soviets'] three years' boycott had been the crudest form of pressure against the independence of the Secretary-General, and the most flagrant violation of Article 100 of the Charter; and there had been continuous vilification and abuse of me and my staff by the Soviet press since 1950. The central theme of it all had been that the Secretariat was dominated by Americans, and that they and I were in all respects tools of Wall Street and Washington. In the light of such charges, it was indeed ironic that the Secretariat should have been subjected at the same time to attacks in the United States for exactly opposite reasons.[22]

The Soviet Attack

The setting in which the Soviet Union mounted its assault on the Secretary-General in 1960 was very different from that of 1952. The membership of the Organization had almost doubled as a result of the influx of many new nations from the developing areas of the world. These were beginning to wield considerable power in the General Assembly. The tensions between the two super-powers had not abated, but numerous minor crises and at least two major ones—in Hungary and Suez—had been weathered short of catastrophe. The United Nations itself had evolved novel techniques of keeping the peace by interposing buffer forces between the major contestants in the Middle East and in the Congo. The Office of the Secretary-General itself had undergone a significant political evolution since the election of its second incumbent, Dag Hammarskjöld, in 1953. It was this new role of the Secretary-General that prompted the Soviet attack.

Hammarskjöld's background was very different from that of his predecessor. He had been an economist and chairman of the Swedish National Bank as well as Deputy Minister for Foreign Affairs. He had never been a member of a political party and was known to have a "passion for anonymity." In short, he was a civil servant, not a politician. Unlike Lie, Hammarskjöld at first chose not to take overt political initiative. Public diplomacy was replaced by "quiet diplomacy." This is not to say that the ferocity of the East-West struggle left the new Secretary-General untouched. But Mr. Hammarskjöld's approach to political disputes differed in two important respects from that of his predecessor. First, he always attempted to gain authority for his actions from the Security Council or the General Assembly, even though this authority was often broad and vaguely worded. Second, most of his diplomatic maneuvers were carried on behind the scenes, away from the searchlight of publicity. The former habit gained him the confidence of the major powers, while the latter made possible agreements without serious loss of face for any nation. A quick survey of Hammarskjöld's major activities before the Congo crisis erupted reveals how active "quiet" diplomacy can be.

In 1954, the Secretary-General flew to Peking to negotiate the release of eleven American airmen who were interned there as UN personnel. Virtually no publicity was released about the trip, but a year later the airmen were released. In 1956, during the Suez crisis, the Secretary-General improvised the UN Emergency Force which helped restore the *status quo ante bellum* in the Middle East. After his unanimous election to a second five-year term of office, there developed a growing tendency in both the General Assembly and the Security Council to grant the Secretary-General broad powers for the exercise of his "quiet diplomacy." Thus, the Assembly requested Hammarskjöld to facilitate the withdrawal of foreign troops during the Lebanese crisis in 1958. And when, in mid-1960, the Belgian withdrawal from the Congo left the new republic strife-torn and threatened by superpower intervention on the model of the Spanish Civil War, the talents of the Secretary-General were called upon once more. Acting under the authority of the Security Council, he organized a United Nations Force, excluding the superpowers, which was to restore peace and order in the Congo until responsible self-government could be established. When the Congo was threatened by civil war through the secession of the province of Katanga, Hammarskjöld—again after securing Security Council authorization—entered Katanga at the head of the UN Force to prevent a major conflagration.

As the Congo crisis developed further, however, Hammarskjöld began to run into major difficulties. A power struggle erupted between the two leading political figures in the Congo—President Joseph Kasavubu and Premier Patrice Lumumba. Kasavubu, conservative and mildly pro-Western, "dismissed" Lumumba, and Lumumba—radical, volatile, and virulently anticolonial—in turn "dismissed" Kasavubu. The Secretary-General refused to embroil the United Nations in this internal struggle, but the superpowers took opposing sides, the United States throwing its support behind Kasavubu and the Soviet Union behind Lumumba.

The Soviet Union had attempted to shore up Lumumba's position by sending transport planes, trucks, and arms. The Secretary-General requested that these shipments cease, since they were contravening his plan to insulate the Congo from superpower involvement. When Andrew W. Cordier, Hammarskjöld's special representative in the Congo, decided to close airports and radio stations in order to prevent the spread of inflammatory propaganda and the extension of civil war, the Soviet Union again accused the Secretary-General of neocolonialism. And when, in early September 1960, Ceylon and Tunisia proposed a resolution in the Security Council that "no assistance for military purposes be sent to the Congo except as part of the UN action," the Soviet Union vetoed it.[23] Thus, the stage was set for a massive attack by the Soviet Union against the Office and person of the Secretary-General.[24]

The Fifteenth Session of the General Assembly opened in September 1960 with a gathering of heads of states unprecedented since the days of the Congress of Vienna. The two superpowers were also represented by their respective national leaders. On September 22, President Eisenhower fully endorsed the actions of the Secretary-General in the Congo. But on the following day, Premier Khrushchev led the Soviet assault.

The Soviet Premier claimed that the Secretary-General was pro-Western and that the United Nations Executive was not representative of the true balance of forces in the world. He declared that Hammarskjöld was abusing the prerogatives of his Office, and that the Congo Force was aiding the aims of the colonialists. Finally, he urged the replacement of the Secretary-Generalship with a three-man directorate:

. . . The conditions appear to be ripe for abolishing the post of Secretary-General, who is now the sole administrator of the Office, the sole interpreter and executor of Security Council and General Assembly decisions. . . .

It is necessary that the executive agency of the United Nations reflect the actual situation now obtaining in the world. The United Nations includes member states of the military blocs of the Western powers, socialist states and neutralist countries. . . .

We deem it wise and fair that the United Nations executive agency consist not of one person, the Secretary-General, but of three persons enjoying the confidence of the United Nations—representatives of the states belonging to the three basic groups mentioned above.

In short, we think that it would be wise to replace the Secretary-General, who is now the sole interpreter and executor of the decisions of the Assembly and the Security Council, by a collective U.N. executive agency consisting of three persons, each representing a definite group of states. This would provide a definite guarantee that the activity of the U.N. executive agency would not prove detrimental to one of these groups of states. The U.N. executive agency would then be a truly democratic body; it would truly safeguard the interests of all U.N. member states, irrespective of their social and political systems.[25]

This "troika" proposal, as it was quickly dubbed, was immediately seen by most of the assembled delegates as a thinly disguised attempt to emasculate the Office of the Secretary-General. A three-man directorate in which each triumvir would have a veto over the actions of the Organization would clearly reduce UN effectiveness to the lowest common denominator. It would extend the veto power into the Secretariat and turn it into a kind of "super Security Council." Moreover, it would make it possible for one of the triumvirs to interrupt a UN operation in midstream, something which had never been possible before. Finally, the division of the triumvirate into three "camps" seemed not only arbitrary and imprecise but would mean that the three Secretaries-General would merely reflect the cold war rather than try to transcend it.

On the whole, the "troika" seemed the perfect formula for total paralysis.

Hammarskjöld's reply to Khrushchev's invitation to "resign in a chivalrous manner" was dignified and eloquent. He stated that he was not beholden primarily to the great powers, but "to all the others" who depended upon a strong and effective United Nations. He told the Assembly that he would rather see the Office of the Secretary-General "break on strict adherence to the principles of independence, impartiality, and objectivity than drift on the basis of compromise."[26] He noted that it would be easier to resign than to resist the assault of the Soviet Union, but declared that his resignation would mean a Soviet veto of any successor and thus the end of an effective UN executive. "The man does not count, the institution does," he concluded.

The Assembly affirmed the Secretary-General's stand with a resounding vote of confidence of 83 in favor, 11 against, and 5 abstentions. The Soviet proposal did receive some consideration from the new nations. Premier Nkrumah of Ghana offered a plan to equip the Secretary-General with three deputies, chosen from the East, West, and neutralist blocs, each with "clearly defined authority" in UN affairs. This would have meant the introduction of the "troika" at a somewhat lower level. And Prime Minister Nehru of India proposed an advisory committee from different geographic areas, a sort of inner cabinet whose views and perhaps even approval would have to be sought on any important matters. None of these suggestions was adopted, however. The United States in particular hoped that the "troika" was dead. But a Moscow editorial noted that "the seeds have been sown and would bear fruit." The Soviet Union had not abandoned its plan, but merely postponed its attack until a more propitious moment.

The announcement of the murder of Patrice Lumumba in Katanga province in February 1961 brought forth a renewed Soviet attack on the United Nations in general and on the Secretary-General in particular. On a level of vituperation rarely matched even by previous Soviet attacks, the Secretary-General was held personally responsible for Lumumba's murder. The USSR demanded that the Congo Force be withdrawn within a month and called for the removal of "Dag Hammarskjöld from the Office of

Secretary-General as an accomplice and organizer of the murder of leading statesmen of the Congo Republic, who [had] stained the name of the United Nations." For its part, "the Soviet Government [would] not maintain any relations with Hammarskjöld and [would] not recognize him as an official of the United Nations."[27]

Hammarskjöld now found himself in the position of former Secretary-General Trygve Lie, from whom the Soviets had also withdrawn recognition when his actions had gone against their will. Nevertheless, Hammarskjöld repeated his pledge of October 3, 1960, not to resign so long as the uncommitted countries wished him to remain.[28] The USSR not only continued its attacks on the Secretary-General, but now broadened its "troika" proposal to cover the Secretariat as a whole. Insisting that there were "no neutral men," the Soviet Union demanded greater Afro-Asian and Soviet representation in the Secretariat, particularly at the higher levels. The United States stood solidly behind the Secretary-General.

Dag Hammarskjöld presented his own political testament in the Introduction to his last Annual Report in August 1961. He distinguished between two views of the United Nations: the organization could be conceived as a "static conference machinery," or it could be a "dynamic instrument" that could take executive action and resolve or forestall conflicts. In his Report, he clearly favored the latter view, thus rejecting the implications of the "troika." Khrushchev responded by stating that "even if all the countries of the world adopted a decision that did not accord with the interests of the Soviet Union, the Soviet Union would not recognize such a decision but would uphold its rights, relying on force."[29]

The tragic death of Dag Hammarskjöld on the eve of the opening of the Sixteenth General Assembly not only plunged most of the delegates into profound grief, but caused considerable anxiety, since the Soviet Union had a veto over the election of a successor. Actually, however, the Soviet leadership was quite aware that it could not get the "troika" plan through the Assembly, but hopeful that it would be able to effect a drastic cutback in the power of the Office by holding out for a modified triumvirate—

the rotation of the Secretary-Generalship among three under-secretaries representing the major blocs.

The United States now attempted to rally the General Assembly behind its view that the Secretary-General's authority must not be compromised and that a single person be named in an acting capacity until a new Secretary-General could be elected. President Kennedy expressed this view forcefully before the Assembly:

> However difficult it may be to fill Mr. Hammarskjöld's place, it can better be filled by one man rather than by three. Even the three horses of the troika did not have three drivers, all going in different directions. They had only one, and so must the United Nations executive. To install a triumvirate, or any rotating authority, in the United Nations administrative offices would replace order with anarchy, action with paralysis, and confidence with confusion.[30]

In response, the Soviet Union, on September 27, proposed that the post of Secretary-General be left vacant and that four under-secretaries—from the United States, the Soviet Union, Africa, and Asia—collectively take charge of the functions of the Office, rotating a temporary chairmanship among themselves. This plan found little, if any, support in the Assembly.

Most of the membership supported a single successor, to be elected in the customary manner. On October 1, the Soviet Union backed down another step and suggested a compromise in which an acting Secretary-General would be elected who would operate "in the spirit of accord" with three under-secretaries, one from each political bloc. This "lower level troika" also found no support. Finally, in intense negotiations between U.S. Ambassador Adlai Stevenson and Soviet Ambassador Valerian Zorin, it was agreed that the under-secretaries would have no veto over the Secretary-General's actions, and that—since no exact number of under-secretaries could be agreed upon—the Secretary-General himself would choose a limited number *after* his election to serve as his principal advisors. This selection was to be based on geographic distribution rather than on ideological blocs. On November 3, 1961, the General Assembly, upon recommendation of the Security Council, unanimously named U Thant of Burma Acting Secretary-General for the remainder of Hammarskjöld's term.

This decision postponed the "troika" issue until April 10, 1963, when Hammarskjöld's term of office was to expire. But Soviet reservations about Acting Secretary-General U Thant apparently were dispelled by his conciliatory mediation during the Cuban crisis of 1962. After private superpower negotiations, the Security Council unanimously recommended, and the General Assembly unanimously approved, the election of U Thant to a full term as Secretary-General retroactive, according to his own wish, to his designation as Acting Secretary-General on November 3, 1961.

Three possible explanations suggest themselves for the Soviet relinquishment of the "troika" plan. In the first place, the proposal found little or no support among the uncommitted nations, and the Soviets were fearful of defying the wishes of that large and influential group of nations most of which happened to agree with the American point of view. Second, UN policy in the Congo after Hammarskjöld's death was run by the "Congo Club," headed by two American Secretariat officials—Ralph Bunche and Andrew Cordier—who simply continued the Secretary-General's policy in the Congo. The Soviets probably thought that a neutralist Acting Secretary-General might be more tractable than leadership of the Secretariat by American officials for an indefinite period. Finally, the Soviet Union retained the power to veto the election of a permanent Secretary-General after the expiration of Hammarskjöld's term. All in all, however, the appointment of U Thant for a full five-year term marked a threefold Soviet concession: "instead of a 'troika,' a single individual was named; he was not required to make any prior commitments to the states sponsoring him; his authority was not circumscribed either by agreement or by the impinging prerogatives of political deputies."[31] The institution of the Office of the Secretary-General as designated under the UN Charter had survived another assault by a superpower.

Conclusions

Both the American and the Soviet attacks on the Secretariat were the result of fear that the Secretary-General was favoring the other superpower. The heart of the position of certain powerful

American critics in the early 1950's was the contention that U.S. nationals of questionable loyalty in the UN Secretariat were helping the Communist cause, while the heart of the Soviet position in the early 1960's was the insistence that the Secretary-General was supporting an American policy in the Congo. Each superpower saw the influence of the other in the actions of the Secretariat and each attacked that institution in an attempt to protect its national interest.

The differences between the two attacks, however, are perhaps more significant than the similarities. First, the sources of the attacks were different. The American executive did not mount the assault as an act of U.S. policy, but permitted the United Nations to be exposed to the pressure of extremist elements in Congress and did little to protect the integrity of the Secretariat. The "troika" proposal, on the other hand, clearly emanated from the Soviet government as an official act of national policy. Second, the goals of the superpowers differed. The United States never questioned the institution of the UN chief executive, although the Congress was prepared to infringe on the independence of the international civil service. The Soviet Union, however, wanted not only to remove the incumbent Secretary-General, but to emasculate the Office. Third, the circumstances of the two cases were entirely different. One involved personnel policy and affected few if any UN members besides the United States; the other was a frontal attack on the very institution of the Secretary-General and aroused the passions of most of the membership. Finally, the United States basically won its battle, whereas the Soviet Union lost, a fact that provides an interesting illustration of the relative power positions of the superpowers in the United Nations at these two different periods. In 1952, the American government was the host country, the largest financial contributor, commanded a two-thirds majority in the General Assembly, and fought its battle on an issue that most members regarded as a private matter between the United States and the United Nations. In 1960 and 1961, the Soviet Union, on the other hand, confronted an enlarged Assembly with a proposal that affected everyone and that, according to most members, had no basis in the Charter.

Perhaps most important, however, is the fact that the UN Secretariat has not only weathered both attacks, but has grown in strength and stature. The battle over personnel policy has largely subsided. The principle of independence of the Secretariat has been reaffirmed and UN personnel policy no longer has the haphazard quality of the early days. Similarly, the "troika" has been shelved and the capacity of the Secretary-General as a political mediator and international statesman has continued to evolve. In short, at times both superpowers have been involved in attacks on the Secretariat in order to protect their national interests, but in each case the negative effect was temporary. Indeed, a case may be made for the proposition that, particularly in the Soviet affair, the attack provided the momentum for a subsequent reaffirmation of the integrity of the Secretariat by a large majority of member states, which left the Office with stronger and more articulate support than before.

SELECTED BIBLIOGRAPHY

Bailey, Sydney D. *The Secretariat of the United Nations.* New York: Carnegie Endowment for International Peace, 1962.

Foote, Wilder T., ed. *Dag Hammarskjöld, Servant of Peace.* New York and Evanston: Harper & Row, 1962.

Gordenker, Leon. *The UN Secretary-General and the Maintenance of Peace.* New York: Columbia University Press, 1967.

Lash, Joseph P. *Dag Hammarskjold: Custodian of the Brushfire Peace.* New York: Doubleday, 1961.

Lie, Trygve. *In the Cause of Peace.* New York: Macmillan, 1954.

Schwebel, Stephen M. *The Secretary-General of the United Nations.* Cambridge, Mass.: Harvard University Press, 1952.

PART II

The Superpowers
and the United Nations
Peace and Security
Operations

CHAPTER 4

———— •◆◆◆• ————

The Middle East Crises
of 1956 and 1967
and the United Nations
Emergency Force

The United States has a strong navy in the zone of the Mediterranean. The Soviet Union also has a strong navy and a powerful air force. The joint and immediate use of these means by the United States and the Soviet Union according to a decision by the United Nations would be a sure guaranty of ending the aggression against the Egyptian people, against the people of the Arab East.

> *Letter from Soviet Premier Bulganin*
> *to President Eisenhower,*
> *November 5, 1956.*

The President has just received a letter from Chairman Bulganin which had been previously released to the press in Moscow. This letter—in an obvious attempt to divert world attention from the Hungarian tragedy—makes the unthinkable suggestion that the United States join with the Soviet Union in a bi-partite employment of their military forces to stop the fighting in Egypt.

> *Response by the White House*
> *to Chairman Bulganin's letter,*
> *November 5, 1956.*

Perhaps the most important responsibility of the United Nations lies in its avowed intention, proclaimed in the Charter, "to save succeeding generations from the scourge of war." The United Nations has already had considerable experience with a variety of peace and security operations, a great deal more, in fact, than the League of Nations had during its entire lifetime. All of them have been distinctive, and few generalizations are possible about them as a group. There was the Korean "police action" in the early 1950's, which actually was a war fought to a stalemate. UNEF in 1956 was the first international peace force, followed soon by ONUC, the far more ambitious and complex experiment in peace-keeping in the Congo. In 1964, the Security Council dispatched a peace force to Cyprus. In addition, the United Nations has sent into the field a number of "Observers" and "Presences": Kashmir, Palestine, Lebanon, Laos, and Yemen are only some of the places which have benefited from these minor peace-keeping operations. There has been, indeed, a permanent procession of such activities, created and directed by the world organization.

In all of these experiments in peace-keeping, the superpowers have been involved either directly or indirectly. Our analysis will limit itself to the interaction between the superpowers in two of the most significant of these operations mounted by the United Nations: the UN Emergency Force in the Middle East and the Congo Force. Since the problem of financing these two forces almost bankrupted the United Nations, and since the dispute between the superpowers over payments was mainly responsible for this, the final chapter of Part II concludes with an analysis of that crisis.

The Middle East Crises
of 1956 and 1967 and the Superpowers

One of the strangest phases in the relationship between the two superpowers occurred in the winter of 1956 in the Middle East. During that "winter of discontent" three different yet interrelated struggles were approaching a climax: the hostility between Israel and the Arab states was escalating toward open combat; the new nationalism of Egypt was becoming increasingly belligerent toward Anglo-French colonialism; and the competition between the Soviet Union and the United States overarched the entire Middle East. The crisis was precipitated in the summer of 1956, when President Gamal Abdel Nasser of Egypt nationalized the Suez Canal Co., abrogating in the eyes of Britain and France the International Convention of Constantinople of 1888, which had provided that "the Suez Maritime Canal shall always be free and open, in time of war as in time of peace, to every vessel of commerce or of war without distinction of flag." The Egyptian leader defended his act by stating that the Canal was within Egyptian territory and that the time had come to announce Egypt's "Declaration of Independence from Imperialism." In an emotional speech, he hailed the nationalization as a symbolic act which would set Arab nationalism on its course from the Atlantic to the Persian Gulf. Britain and France, aghast at this unexpected move, lodged a strong protest against the seizure of "an international waterway" and against the violation of what the two Western nations considered to be their legal rights in the area. For Britain, as well as for Egypt, the Suez Canal was a symbol. While for Egypt it represented the growing power of the new nationalism, for Britain control of the Canal symbolized her status as an Empire and as a world power. To the French, who blamed Egypt for supporting the Algerian rebellion against France, seizure of the Canal served as a last straw. For Britain and France alike, the issue at stake was not merely the rational one of safeguarding the economic rights of their shareholders in the Suez Canal Company or of protecting a key economic life line. Far more important was their emotional reaction to the seemingly insolent nationalism represented by the Egyptian move. Thus, the stage was set for a violent encounter between nationalism and colonialism.

During the weeks that followed Nasser's action the conflict broadened. Britain and France sounded out the official American reaction to the situation. Prime Ministers Eden and Mollet, contemplating the use of force against Nasser, were partially reassured by the fact that Secretary of State Dulles also appeared outraged by Egypt's action. The British and French Foreign Ministers compared Nasser's action to Hitler's behavior at Munich and stated in the strongest terms that this type of Western appeasement must not be allowed to occur again. Secretary Dulles replied that "force was the last method to be tried, but the United States did not exclude the use of force if all other methods failed."[1] From this statement Eden inferred that the United States would, at best, present a united front with Britain and France in a show of force against Nasser and, at worst, remain benevolently neutral.

Britain and France now prepared for military action. They hoped to mount a lightning attack against Egypt, occupy the Canal, depose Nasser, and then negotiate with his successor from a position of strength. In the course of these preparations, it became increasingly evident to the two Western powers that they shared a common interest with Israel. The new Jewish state, harassed by border clashes and made increasingly insecure by Nasser's pronouncements "to drive Israel into the sea," could be used as the cutting edge of the Anglo-French punitive expedition against Egypt. "Collusion" between Britain and France on the one hand and Israel on the other has not been substantiated, but circumstantial evidence points in that direction. At any rate, Israel invaded Egyptian territory on October 29, 1956, and rapidly advanced toward the Suez Canal. On the following day, Britain and France issued an ultimatum to Israel and Egypt calling for a cessation of fighting and demanding the occupation of Suez and other key areas. The ultimatum was rejected by Egypt, and on October 31, British and French airplanes bombarded Cairo. What had begun as an armed conflict between two Middle Eastern nations now assumed the proportions of a direct Western attack against the new nationalism.

The superpowers entered the picture on October 30. On that day, the United States called for a meeting of the Security Council and, to the consternation of Britain and France, introduced a resolution calling upon Israel to leave Egypt without delay and asking all member states to "refrain from the use of force or threat of force."[2] This resolution was immediately vetoed by Britain and France. At the same meeting, the Soviet Union asked the Security Council to pass a draft incorporating some parts of the defeated U.S.-sponsored resolution. China and Iran suggested adding still other parts of the defeated resolution and the USSR agreed. At the next meeting, the Council voted on the Soviet-Chinese-Iranian draft. Again this proposal was vetoed by Britain and France.[3]

As the Security Council stood paralyzed and the Anglo-French action continued, the tension between the superpowers mounted steadily. Premier Bulganin, in a news conference in Moscow, warned of the possibility of a third world war and declared that Soviet "volunteers" were ready to aid the Egyptian forces. He proposed that the United States and the Soviet Union restore the peace in the Middle East through a joint show of force. This suggestion was rejected as "unthinkable" by President Eisenhower. Simultaneously, a Soviet draft resolution proposing a joint U.S.-Soviet force to be established under Article 42 was rejected by the Security Council under strong American pressure.[4] The United States was eager to see the Anglo-French action ended, but it was equally eager to prevent the establishment of a Soviet presence in the Middle East.

On November 1, the Security Council, at the instigation of the Yugoslav delegation, invoked the "Uniting for Peace" procedure and called an emergency session of the General Assembly. The United States and the Soviet Union both supported this move, and only Britain and France cast negative votes. In the Assembly, on November 2, the United States adopted a sternly condemnatory attitude toward the Anglo-French military action. "The United States," declared President Eisenhower, "was not consulted in any way about any phase of these actions, nor were we informed of them in advance."[5] Secretary of State Dulles condemned the resort to force by Britain and France, and Israel, which could "scarcely be reconciled with the principles and purposes of the United Nations to which we have all subscribed."[6] In this attitude, the United States found support from a not particularly welcome source—the Soviet Union.

The USSR, in a vehement denunciation of the Anglo-French action, urged the Assembly "to condemn the armed attack by the United Kingdom, France, and Israel against Egypt as an act of aggression incompatible with the purposes and principles of the United Nations; to demand the immediate cessation of hostilities and the withdrawal of armed forces; and to appoint a United Nations commission to supervise the carrying out of the recommendations of the General Assembly."[7]

The two superpowers were able to agree on a compromise resolution sponsored by the United States, urging a cease-fire, and a withdrawal of all forces behind the armistice lines. The resolution was adopted by a vote of 64 in favor, 5 opposed, and 6 abstentions. One of those abstaining was Lester Pearson of Canada, who claimed that the resolution had made "one great omission": it had not provided for a vital instrument to prevent another explosion in the Suez area—"a truly international peace and police force."[8] After sounding out key delegations and the Secretary-General, Mr. Pearson, on November 3, introduced a draft resolution requesting the Secretary-General to submit a plan within forty-eight hours for the creation, "with the consent of the nations concerned," of an emergency international force "to secure and supervise the cessation of hostilities." The United States gave the plan its strong support, declaring that it was interested in a solution that would "meet the immediate crisis as well as do something that would go to the causes and into the more long-range subjects."[9] The Soviet Union felt that more coercive action would be preferable, but did not object strongly to the Canadian plan. Thus, the General Assembly, on November 3, approved the Canadian draft resolution by a vote of 57 to 0, with 19 abstentions.[10] The abstainers included the Soviet bloc, Britain, France, Israel, Egypt, Australia, New Zealand, the Union of South Africa, Portugal, Austria, and Laos.

Thus, the United States, instead of observing a benevolent neutrality toward the British, French, and Israeli actions, had taken a leading role in the General Assembly in calling for a cessation of fighting and the immediate withdrawal of the Anglo-French-Israeli forces from Egypt. To the consternation of many of its allies in NATO, the United States found itself side by side in the United Nations with its great antagonist in the East-West struggle. Thus, under joint pressure of the superpowers in the Assembly, Britain had to yield. Confronted by UN resolutions charging her with aggression, dismayed by the actions of the United States, and troubled by an increasingly hostile opposition at home, Prime Minister Eden terminated his abortive venture. France had no choice but to follow suit, and the "gentle persuasion" of the United States resulted in the withdrawal of Israeli forces shortly thereafter. As Secretary-General Hammarskjöld set about improvising an international peace force, most delegates in the General Assembly felt that a world conflagration had narrowly been averted.

If one takes stock of the roles the superpowers played in the Suez crisis up to this point, it is apparent that the United States faced the most difficult choice: What action did its national interest dictate? Where did its national interest really lie? It was confronted in the most acute way possible with the dilemma of whether to support the colonial powers or the new nationalism. Its actual decision to side with Egypt inevitably alienated Britain and France and put the most severe strains on the NATO alliance. Sir Anthony Eden was compelled to resign and throughout Britain as well as France a growing body of anti-American sentiment became vocal. Indeed, in the view of a number of observers, such as former Secretary of State Dean Acheson, American policy in the crisis came close to losing the United States its two closest allies, splitting the NATO alliance, and thus exposing Western Europe to the domination of Communism.[11] On the other hand, if the United States had sided with Britain and France against Egypt, its risks would have been no less heavy. The new nations of Africa, Asia, and the Middle East would have quickly concluded that when the chips were down the United States was at heart no less a colonial power than its Western Europe allies. In disillusionment, the new nationalism would have veered away from the United States toward the Soviet Union. Probably the least amount of animosity would have resulted if the United States had abstained from the conflict altogether. Yet even then both sides would likely have found reason for objecting to America's role.

As one observer has pointed out, "the criticism of the American stand came essentially to this point: the United States had chosen to behave like a collective security power, not like an ally. In the Middle Eastern situation, Uniting for Peace had prevailed over NATO."[12] Yet, the American rejection as "unthinkable" of a Soviet proposal for joint superpower intervention in the Middle East suggests strongly that the American position was not determined by the abstract considerations of the collective-security ideal. There was, first, a sense of outrage, felt by both the President and Secretary of State because the British and French had not bothered to consult their NATO ally on so important a matter as military action in the Middle East. Second, from a purely military standpoint, the punitive expedition seemed to be foundering and thus could not be presented to the General Assembly as a *fait accompli*. The United States, by supporting the Anglo-French venture or even by taking a neutral view of it, would have risked the ill-will of a large majority of the UN membership and, in addition, would have been in an embarrassing position if the military action failed or bogged down. Most important, the United States feared the intervention of the Soviet Union in the Middle East through "volunteers" and the risk of sparking a major war through direct superpower confrontation in the contested area.

All this does not deny the possibility that some of the reasons which motivated the United States may have been of a genuinely moral nature. As the American government stated, the United States acted as it did because it insisted on the principle that the same standard of international law and morality should apply to all nations, friends and foes alike. Yet even this seemingly unassailable moral reason rested upon ambiguities. It could be argued, for example, that a "moral" action might under certain circumstances result in "immoral" consequences. Thus the "moral" behavior of the United States in the Suez Crisis ran the risk of leading to the disintegration of NATO and the "immoral" result of opening Western Europe to Soviet pressure. Conversely, if the United States had decided upon the "immoral" step of supporting the British and French military expedition against Egypt, the outcome might have been the quite "moral" one of restoring the legal economic rights of the Western powers and of reestablishing the Suez Canal as an international waterway. The point here is *not* that the United States acted either morally or immorally. It is, rather, that among other things, the Suez affair demonstrated how subtle and indeterminate the relationship between ethics and power in international relations can be.

The Soviet Union's national interest in the Suez crisis was much easier to determine. From its point of view, the only unusual aspect was its alliance with the United States in the United Nations. In order to dissociate itself from this somewhat unwelcome association, the Soviet Union interpreted the action of the United States not as helpful to Arab nationalism but, rather, as a nefarious scheme to replace British and French imperialism with American imperialism. In contrast, it pointed to itself as the only true champion of the new nationalist cause. The Soviet offer of "volunteers" was designed to underline its firm commitment to the new nationalism. Indeed, from the Soviet Union's point of view, the Suez crisis constituted a great windfall in the East-West struggle: the British and French appeared to be digging their own graves in the Middle East and the United States seemed to be doing its best to help them. Thus, by appealing to the cause of Arab nationalism, the Soviet Union saw its opportunity to eject Western influence from the Middle East and gain a foothold of its own. The fact that Israel was allied with the two colonial powers made it easier for the Soviet Union to inflame Arab nationalism. Typically, therefore, the Soviet Union showed itself ready to use every facet of this colonial struggle to advance its own cause in the East-West battle. From the melee, Communism emerged with a clear-cut gain.

The main losers in the Suez affair were clearly the two colonial powers, Britain and France. In humiliation, they had to watch Nasser snatch a political victory from a military defeat. Abandoned by their traditional ally, they had to admit that they could no longer act like great powers and that, in the last analysis, their initiative in international politics depended upon the decision of the United States. The new nationalism had inflicted a painful defeat upon them and the very issue which they had set out to rectify by force of arms—the internationalization of the Suez Canal —now seemed beyond redemption. For all practical purposes, the Suez crisis terminated Anglo-French authority in the Middle East. Suez had become another Dienbienphu.

The greatest victory in the Suez crisis was won by Arab nationalism. Nasser now was clearly master of the Suez Canal. The two great superpowers had both supported him. The prestige of the Egyptian leader reached its zenith immediately after the Suez affair, although it was somewhat tarnished by the military disaster of Egyptian arms. Not only did Nasser triumph in the showdown with Western colonialism, but his other great foe, Israel, had also been compelled to withdraw as a result of American pressure. The political logic of the East-West struggle, by becoming the decisive factor in the crisis, thus operated to advance the cause of Arab nationalism to greater strength and prestige than it had ever possessed or than Nasser could ever have hoped to gain on his own.

Israel emerged with certain important gains: it had demonstrated its military superiority over Nasser. Yet, it was prevented from capitalizing on its advantage by strong U.S. pressure to withdraw. In the end, all the territories it had occupied had to be given up.

While each state in the Suez crisis had its national interest to protect, each actor was also a participant in the three-struggle pattern outlined above. What were the results there? In the East-West struggle, the Soviet Union clearly had come off best. It had created a more attractive image of itself in the Arab world. The promulgation by the United States of the Eisenhower Doctrine in March 1957—pledging American assistance against Communism to Middle Eastern countries—was testimony to increasing American awareness of this latest Soviet gain. In the second struggle, that of nationalism versus colonialism, the winner was clearly the new nationalism. After Suez, the great-power role of Britain and France in the Middle East was clearly at an end. The Eisenhower Doctrine attempted to salvage what was left of Anglo-French influence. In the third struggle, between Arab nationalism and Israeli nationalism, both countries emerged stronger from the crisis: Israel because of its formidable military prowess, Egypt because of its political triumph over Britain and France.

Interdependence among the major actors again was the keynote of the Arab-Israeli war of 1967, although the specific alignment of forces was quite different. This time the two superpowers took opposing sides, while Britain tended to favor Israel and France leaned toward the Arabs.

The decade between the two crises had seen a number of border incidents but no major eruption. In early 1967, however, tension began to mount. President Nasser's Arab neighbors accused the Egyptian leader of hiding behind the UN Emergency Force in order to avoid a confrontation with Israel. Sensitive to this charge, on May 18, Nasser demanded that UNEF leave the positions in Sinai that it had occupied for more than ten years.

Whether the Egyptian leader initiated this move primarily to assuage his Arab critics or whether he really intended to clear the field for military action is not certain. At any rate, Secretary-General U Thant complied with the demand, reasoning that UNEF could no longer remain in the area if the consent of the host government were withdrawn. Hence the UNEF contingents were removed from Sinai, the Gaza strip, and from Sharm El-Sheik overlooking the Straits of Tiran. Almost simultaneously, Israel, Syria, and Jordan began to mobilze their armed forces and to mass them on their respective borders. On May 20, military control over the Gaza Strip reverted to Egypt, and the Arab League issued a joint declaration that was signed by twelve of its members, with only Tunisia abstaining, stating that an attack on one would be considered an attack upon all. Israel responded by calling up the reserves, and on May 22, Egypt ordered total mobilization. During this early phase of the crisis, the superpowers indicated their positions, but still refused to become vitally involved.

The second phase of the crisis began on May 23, when President Nasser announced a blockade of the Gulf of Aqaba, thus cutting off Israel's only southern port, at Elath. Israel immediately responded by defining the blockade as an act of war that entitled it to take appropriate action. Egypt maintained that the Straits of Tiran were within her territorial waters and thus could be closed to states with which she was at war.

At this juncture, the East-West struggle was superimposed upon the competing nationalisms of Israel and the Arab states. On May 23, President Lyndon B. Johnson presented the American position. He described the blockade as "illegal and potentially disastrous to the cause of peace" and affirmed that "the right of free, innocent passage through the international water [was] a vital interest of the international community." In effect, the President supported the settlement that had been reached after the Suez crisis of 1956. Because Egypt was determined to overthrow that settlement, the American position in effect came down on the side of Israel.

On the following day, the Soviet Union declared that Israel

was to blame for the dangerous aggravation of tensions in the Middle East. The forces of imperialism, represented by "a handful of colonial oil monopolies" and backed by commercial interests in the United States and Britain, were the chief culprits behind the scene, in the Soviet view. The USSR further proclaimed its support for the Arab states in their "just struggle for national liberation against colonialism."

The other major powers, Britain, France, and Communist China, also took their stands in the escalating crisis. Britain supported the United States on the right of free passage of all nations through the disputed straits; France declared herself to be "not committed in any way and on any subject" on the side of "any of the states involved;" and China, supporting the Arab cause, also accused both the United States and the Soviet Union of "strangling the just struggle of the Palestinian people."

In the meantime, the two main protagonists edged closer to the brink. On May 25, Israel's Ambassador, Abba Eban, flew to London and Washington in order to ascertain what the two Western powers would do to end the blockade. Both offered vague assurances but counseled restraint. On May 28, Syria and Iraq signed a military agreement calling for the cooperation of their armies against Israel; on the following day, President Nasser announced that Soviet Premier Alexei Kosygin had sent him a pledge to guarantee the Egyptian blockade. On May 30, King Hussein, described several weeks earlier as a "Hashemite Harlot" by President Nasser, placed Jordan's armed forces under Egyptian control in the event of war with Israel. Thus, by the end of May, the brink was reached and Israel confronted the armies of Egypt, Syria, and Jordan.

On the morning of June 5, heavy fighting broke out between Israel and Egypt. In four days of lightning warfare, Israel defeated the armies of her three main Arab antagonists. In Egypt, she captured the Sinai up to the east bank of the Suez Canal and also lifted the blockade of Aqaba by capturing Sharm El-Sheik. The Gaza Strip also fell into Israeli hands. In bloody fighting with Jordan, Israel occupied the Old City of Jerusalem and all of Jordan west of the Jordan River. Finally, Israel also captured portions of Syrian borderlands from which Arab guns had harassed Israeli settlements. On June 9, the short but violent war came to a halt with a cease-fire resolution passed by the UN Security Council.

During the next phase, the conflict moved from the military arena of the Middle East to the political forum of the United Nations. Both the Security Council and the General Assembly debated the issues, the latter in a four-week emergency special session. In the world forum, Israel insisted on recognition by the Arab states and an end to belligerency as conditions of withdrawal from the occupied Arab territories. She was supported in this view by the United States and Britain. The Arab states demanded unconditional withdrawal and full reparations and insisted that Israel be condemned as an aggressor. Soviet Premier Kosygin supported the Arab demands from the rostrum of the General Assembly. France inclined toward the Arab position and the small nations were about evenly divided. Neither superpower was able to muster a two-thirds majority for its respective position, and thus the General Assembly adjourned in a mood of frustration after two resolutions calling upon Israel to rescind its annexation of Old Jerusalem were ignored. The one concrete UN measure was the dispatch of a small number of cease-fire observers to the Suez Canal.

An analysis of the changes in power constellations after the war reveals some suggestive comparisons and contrasts with the 1956 crisis. In the first place, the Soviet Union had backed a loser this time, whereas she had been on the winning side a decade earlier. Most of the military hardware that the USSR had shipped to the Arab states had been captured or destroyed in the four days of war. Nor was the Soviet Union able to turn anticolonial sentiments to its advantage in the United Nations, because many of the smaller nations also identified themselves with Israel. On the other hand, the defeat of the Arab states now made these states more than ever dependent upon the USSR, which promptly resumed arms shipments to them.

The role of the United States was once again problematical. She was on the winning side, and superficially her policy seemed successful. But on a deeper level, it was clear that the swiftness of Israel's victory had saved the United States from having to make some very difficult decisions. Had the war gone badly for

Israel, the United States might have been forced to intervene and risk a confrontation with the Soviet Union.

Britain and France, the two main losers in the 1956 affair, were only marginally involved this time. A new power factor in the equation, however, was Communist China, which accused the United States and the Soviet Union of conspiring together in the Middle East.

Israel, which had to withdraw in 1956, this time was determined not to yield its military gains except in exchange for an end to belligerency. This the Arabs were unwilling to concede, and therefore, in the view of many observers, the 1967 war had exacerbated the deeper causes of the conflict.

Thus, by mid-1967, the balance of power in the Middle East had been definitely altered. Although Israel had won her military victory essentially unaided, the political constellation clearly showed once again the interdependence of the two great struggles of our time. One superpower tried to exploit the Arab-Israeli war by describing it as a struggle between Arab nationalism and Western imperialism. In this effort, the USSR failed where it had succeeded in 1956, when the two superpowers found themselves on the same side. And the United States, eager to pacify the struggle, was saved from the decision to intervene by Israeli arms. Thus, the connection between the two world struggles might have widened the theater of war had the conflict between the two main antagonists been inconclusive or gone the other way.

So far as the United Nations' role in the conflict was concerned, both Israel and the Arab states were profoundly disappointed. Israel perceived the United Nations as hostile and the Arabs tended to regard it as useless. Be that as it may, there was little doubt that —in the light of the numerous Middle East resolutions that had gone unimplemented—the currency of United Nations resolutions was in danger of serious devaluation.

The United States Emergency Force and the Superpowers

The United Nations Emergency Force (UNEF) could not have come into existence without the approval, or at least the tacit consent, of the two superpowers. Yet both were carefully excluded from participation. UNEF was never meant to be a fighting army, but rather a symbol of the UN's involvement which, it was hoped, would bring about the neutralization of the disputed area. The direct involvement of one of the superpowers would have meant the necessity of inviting the other as well. Hence, neither was invited by the Secretary-General, and UNEF thus became the first genuine international peace force not dominated by a great power.

When Secretary-General Hammarskjöld and Lester Pearson began to build the Force, they decided to appoint Major General E. L. M. Burns, chief of staff of the United Nations Truce Supervision Organization in Palestine, as head of the new United Nations Command. The next vital decision concerned the composition of troops to be sent. To the delight of leading UN officials, 24 members agreed to make troops available for the enterprise, with offers ranging from 1,180 from Canada to 250 from Finland. However, this delight began to give way to embarrassment when, in order not to jeopardize relations with Egypt, it became necessary to reject some of the offers. For example, the Canadian contingent, especially a battalion of the "Queen's Own Rifles," resembled the British too much in appearance. Pearson tactfully decided to use them as maintenance and administrative personnel in roles where they would be least conspicuous. New Zealand troops were politely rejected because New Zealand had voted with Britain and France in the General Assembly on the Suez affair. Pakistan was considered unsuitable because it was a member of the Baghdad Pact and an irritant to India. Troops from the Soviet bloc —Czechoslovakia and Rumania—were not "rejected" but simply not "activated." Finally, 6,000 troops from ten countries—Brazil, Canada, Colombia, Denmark, Finland, India, Indonesia, Norway, Sweden, and Yugoslavia—were ready for action.

The composition of the Force was very important, since its admission to the contested area depended upon the permission of Egypt. Though this condition was distasteful to many members of the Assembly as well as to UN officials, it was, according to the Secretary-General, the "very basis and starting point" of the entire operation. In effect, Egypt therefore had a veto over the national make-up of the Force and could, as well, determine the length of its stay in the Suez area. On November 12, Egypt granted UNEF permission to enter. Shortly thereafter, Britain, France, and Israel were persuaded to withdraw from Egyptian territory and UNEF proceeded to neutralize the contested boundary zones. Its function became essentially that of a "buffer" between Israel and Egypt.

The United States fully supported the UNEF experiment, which served the American national interest in two ways: first, the United States was eager to heal the rift between itself and its two NATO allies—Britain and France—and, second, it was equally eager to remove any pretext for unilateral Soviet intervention in the Middle East. Thus, the United States saw its national interest well served by placing the responsibility for a solution in international hands. No American troops were included in UNEF. Had the United States assumed a more active role, the suspicion of the Soviet Union and the Afro-Asian nations would no doubt have been aroused. Hence, American involvement was limited to the marginal one of providing transport planes, uniforms, helmets, and other kinds of material and logistical support for the Force. On the matter of the direction and control of UNEF, the position of the United States was at all times congruent with that of the Secretary-General.

The Soviet view of UNEF has been critical. However, its opposition has always remained muted and never reached the proportions of active obstruction. Part of the criticism has been of a legal nature. The Soviet Union has maintained that only the Security Council, acting under Chapter VII of the Charter, has the power to establish an international police force.[13] The creation of UNEF by the Assembly under the "Uniting for Peace" procedure has therefore come under Soviet fire. On the other hand, in the Suez case, this procedure was invoked by the Assembly to overcome not a Soviet, but a British and French, veto. Hence, while the Soviet Union has in general been deeply hostile to the extension of the Assembly's mandate into the area of peace and security, in this specific instance its national interest dictated abstention on the vote to establish UNEF and only relatively mild criticism thereafter. The USSR was also suspicious of UNEF on political grounds. It had fears that UNEF would permanently remove the Suez Canal from Egyptian control and possibly aid

Britain and France in the goal of reestablishing their authority. And finally, it voiced concern that the Force was an American scheme to displace Anglo-French influence with American power.

In May 1967, President Nasser abruptly demanded that UNEF be withdrawn from the borders that it had patroled for over a decade. Secretary-General U Thant complied with the Egyptian demand, though with serious misgivings, and the Force was promptly removed.

U Thant's decision was a very controversial one. The Secretary-General was widely criticized for giving in too hastily to Egyptian pressure. Critics pointed out that, although it was true that UNEF's presence on the Egyptian border depended on the consent of the Egyptian government, the Secretary-General could have stalled by requesting an emergency session of the Security Council or of the General Assembly and thus gained time. The Israeli Ambassador to the United Nations, Abba Eban, stated caustically that "the umbrella was removed at the precise moment when it began to rain." The Secretary-General defended his action by pointing out that there would have been no legal basis for maintaining the Force on Egyptian soil without that nation's consent. Moreover, the Force had never been permitted to patrol the Israeli side of the border, and when the Israeli government was asked whether it would invite the UNEF troops to its side after they left Egypt, Israel replied that it would refuse to do so. Both governments were within their legal rights, the Secretary-General asserted. A further complication in the picture was the fact that two nations that had given contingents to UNEF—India and Yugoslavia—were removing their forces even before the Secretary-General had given the order to withdraw. Moreover, several UNEF soldiers were killed by Egyptian troops with the threat that, unless UNEF was promptly withdrawn, it would be regarded as an "army of occupation." Finally, the Secretary-General reasoned that if he did not comply with the request of a sovereign government, consent for the admission of a peace-keeping force in a future crisis might be infinitely more difficult to obtain. Given all these conflicting considerations, the Secretary-General made his difficult and fateful choice.

Conclusions

The escalation of the Suez crisis of 1956 may be seen in three concentric circles: the crisis began between two competing forms of nationalism—Arab and Israeli; when Britain and France attacked Egypt in retaliation against President Nasser's nationalization of the Suez Canal, the local struggle merged into the larger one of nationalism versus colonialism; and immediately thereafter, the superpower conflict entered the picture. The speed of the escalation process impressed the need for UN action upon the membership, and the involvement of the superpowers in the crisis made it clear that their political support for, or at least acquiescence in, such action would be essential. Yet, given the explosiveness of the situation, it seemed best to exclude them from actual physical participation. These twin premises became the basis of UNEF.

The UNEF experience demonstrated that the United Nations was capable of responding to a major challenge with extraordinary resourcefulness. The framers of the Charter had assumed that concerted military action by the great powers would nip any conflict in the bud. Actually, however, in the Suez crisis the peace depended not on how quickly the superpowers' armed forces would be brought to the scene, but on how successfully they could be kept at arm's length. Neither superpower was asked to contribute troops to UNEF. The United Nations adjusted its peacekeeping machinery to the original intentions of the Charter.

The abstention of the superpowers from active participation in UNEF points up a striking dilemma for any international force. In order to be an effective instrument of collective security and a powerful military force, it must include one or more of the great powers. But if it does, it is likely to find itself dominated by a superpower, as was the case in Korea, and to suffer a proportionate loss of its international character. Hence, a truly international force that excludes the superpowers can hardly be more than a "buffer," or at best "an intermediary technique between merely passing resolutions and actually fighting."[14]

Despite the fact that the superpowers were excluded from

actual peace-keeping activities in UNEF, the success of the operation largely depended upon their political attitudes. The United States gave UNEF its strong support from beginning to end and the Soviet Union, though highly ambivalent about the Force, never actively obstructed its operations. Thus the General Assembly and the Secretary-General were able to conduct the action in a relatively smooth manner until the withdrawal of the Force in 1967.

In a more fundamental sense, however, the differing relations of the superpowers in 1956 and 1967 vitally affected the capacity of the United Nations to deal with the two crises. In 1956, the fact that the United States and the Soviet Union found themselves temporarily on the same side contributed in large measure to the passage of the Assembly resolution authorizing the establishment of UNEF. In 1967, the fact that the superpowers were clearly on opposite sides prevented the world organization from playing more than a marginal role in the conflict. The year 1956 thus proved that superpower opposition need not rule out the possibility of effective UN action so long as such opposition remains relatively passive. The year 1967 proved, however, that once superpower competition assumes a more virulent and active form, the United Nations cannot be an effective peace-keeping instrument but is more likely to serve as international conference machinery. Thus, despite the growing UN membership and the changing balance of forces in the world organization, the role of the superpowers in the constellation still remains crucial.

SELECTED BIBLIOGRAPHY

Burns, Arthur Lee, and Nina Heathcote. *Peace-Keeping by UN Forces: From Suez to the Congo.* New York: Praeger, 1963.

Claude, Inis L., Jr. "The United Nations and the Use of Force," *International Conciliation*, No. 532 (March 1961).

Frye, William R. *A United Nations Peace Force.* New York: Oceana, 1957.

Goodrich, Leland. *Korea: A Study of United States Policy in the United Nations.* New York: Harper & Row, 1956.

Goodrich, Leland, and Anne Simons. *The United Nations and the Maintenance of Peace and Security.* Washington, D.C.: The Brookings Institution, 1955.

James, Alan. *The Politics of Peace-Keeping.* New York: Frederick A. Praeger, 1969.

Rosner, Gabriella. *The United Nations Emergency Force.* New York: Columbia University Press, 1963.

Wainhouse, David D. *International Peace Observation.* Baltimore: The Johns Hopkins University Press, 1966.

CHAPTER 5

The Congo Crisis and the United Nations Operation in the Congo

Does independence come wrapped in paper or do we get it at the bank?

An anonymous Congolese

Phase One: Superpower Consensus

The Congo crisis of the early 1960's affords a second illuminating case study of superpower interaction in the area of peace and security operations. Historians may differ with Mr. Hammarskjöld's view that the UN's task in the Congo was the most important responsibility that the world organization had to shoulder in the first fifteen years of its lifetime, but most will agree that the Congo problem sorely strained the UN's diplomatic, military, and financial resources. The two superpowers played major roles throughout the entire drama.

Belgian rule in the Congo had for fifty years been based on the assumption that a paternalistic concern for the physical well-being and economic needs of the indigenous population would prevent the rise of a nationalist movement. When, in January 1959, violent nationalist riots erupted in Leopoldville, the Congolese capital, it became clear that this assumption had been incorrect. The Belgian government, interpreting these riots as a harbinger of impending disaster, decided to end its colonial rule as rapidly as possible. Independence for the Congo was slated for June 30, 1960. During the last year of Belgian colonial rule, little attempt was made to prepare an indigenous elite for the imminent responsi-

bilities of self-government. Only a handful of Congolese had enjoyed a university education and the overwhelming majority of
the Congo's fourteen million people were illiterate. Most were
under the impression that on Independence Day all Belgian prop-
erty would revert to the Congolese population. As one Congolese
phrased the question, "Does independence come wrapped in paper
or do we get it at the bank?"[1]

Thus, on June 30, 1960, the colony of the Belgian Congo was
suddenly transformed into an independent nation, a new-born in-
fant left on the world's doorstep. The government that took over
the Congo was headed by President Joseph Kasavubu and Premier Patrice Lumumba. Both had been members of the Congolese
Nationalist Movement. Kasavubu, the more conservative of the
two, was not excessively hostile toward Belgium and the Western
powers. The Office of the Presidency which he came to occupy
was largely an honorific post. Lumumba, the Premier, had been a
more ardent nationalist than Kasavubu, and was resolved to sever
all relations with Belgium after independence. Both these men
were challenged in their views by Moise Tshombe, Premier of the
provincial government of Katanga. Tshombe had been backed by
the Belgian government during the colonial period. He was a
wealthy man, conservative, and pro-Belgian. Thus the new Congolese leadership held political views along the entire spectrum—from
Lumumba's uncompromising anticolonialism to Tshombe's pro-Belgian sentiments.

A few hours after its Declaration of Independence, the new
government faced a crisis which threatened its very survival. The
Congolese Army of 25,000 men, which had never had an African
officer corps, rose up, demanding the ouster of its Belgian officers
and pay increases for the enlisted men. Many disappointed civilians
who had expected to inherit all Belgian possessions on Independence Day joined in the mutiny. During the following days the
mutiny spread through the rest of the Congo. In the major cities
lawlessness prevailed and thousands of Belgians fled. On July 11,
Tshombe declared that Katanga was seceding from the rest of the
country and forming a new state allied with Belgium. Since Katanga Province was the wealthiest part of the Congo, possessing
the country's richest mineral deposits, this act of secession threat-

ened the life of the new state. Moreover, the provincial government of Katanga requested Belgian military help in order to suppress the violence that was engulfing it along with the rest of the Congo. Belgian troops reentered Katanga for the purpose of restoring order. But on the following day, the Belgian government charged that since the new Congolese government of Premier Lumumba had been unable to protect the lives and interests of the remaining Belgian population, Belgian troops would march into Leopoldville as well. When the Belgians reentered the capital, shooting broke out between them and Congolese soldiers. At this point the Lumumba regime began to blame the riots not on the Africans but on the Belgians. The Premier accused Belgium of aggression and stated that the colonial power had conspired with Tshombe to engineer the secession of Katanga Province in order to find a justification for the reimposition of colonial rule. What had started as only a local conflict thus quickly took on the dimensions of a major struggle between nationalism and colonialism.

On July 13, 1960, members of the Lumumba regime cabled the United States government for aid, but both Premier Lumumba and President Kasavubu immediately disavowed this appeal and stated that it had been meant as a request for a UN force composed of military personnel from neutral countries. Nevertheless, the earlier request touched off a sequence of events that turned the Congo into a battleground for the superpowers. Soviet Premier Khrushchev immediately announced that the Congolese soldiers had been perfectly right in their mutiny against the Belgian officers. He also claimed that the United States and the Western colonial powers in NATO had conspired to send Belgian troops into the Congo to reimpose colonial status under the pretext of restoring order. UN Secretary-General Dag Hammarskjöld called an emergency meeting of the Security Council and urged authorization for the dispatching of a UN military force to the Congo. During the Council session the Soviet Union condemned Belgian "armed aggression" and accused the United States of collusion with colonialism. The United States denounced the Soviet accusation as "outrageous and untrue." The Security Council, in an 8-to-o vote, called on Belgium to withdraw its troops from the Congo and authorized the Secretary-General to organize a United Nations

Operation in the Congo—ONUC—to be patterned on the model of the Middle East Force established during the Suez crisis of 1956. Both the Soviet Union and the United States voted for the resolution, while Britain, France, and Nationalist China abstained.

Thus, the first UN resolution on the Congo reflected at least a temporary consensus between the superpowers. It was in the national interest of the United States to interpose the authority of the United Nations between East and West and to prevent the Congo from becoming another battlefield in the cold war; it was in the Soviet interest to speed the withdrawal of the Belgian forces and thus to play its self-appointed role as champion of anticolonialism. As in the Suez case, the ultimately divergent national goals of the two superpowers did not prevent them from permitting common UN action. Moreover, the solid backing of the African states for the resolution encouraged both superpowers to stand clear.

The superpower consensus thus established was tenuous, however. Premier Khrushchev revealed the continuing basic conflict in national interests when he announced that the Soviet Union was considering direct intervention in the Congo. He stated that this might become necessary, since he had received a telegram from President Kasavubu and Premier Lumumba stating that their lives were in danger and that they might "be compelled to ask for intervention by the Soviet Union if the Western camp [did] not desist from aggression against the sovereignty of the Congo Republic."[2] The Soviet leader pledged Russia's support to Lumumba and told the West, "Hands off the Congo!" On July 24, the Soviet delegation to the United Nations demanded the evacuation of the Belgian "aggressors" within three days. The U.S. representative, Henry Cabot Lodge, countered with the declaration that the United States "would do whatever may be necessary to prevent the intrusion of any military forces not requested by the United Nations."[3] The Security Council barred unilateral intervention and urged the speedy withdrawal of Belgian forces. In the meantime, ONUC was gradually replacing the Belgian troops. The two superpowers were carefully excluded from the international contingent. Almost 20,000 troops from twenty-nine nations, including Morocco, Tunisia, Ghana, Ethiopia, Mali, Guinea, Ireland, Sweden, and India—all under the UN flag—were deployed throughout the Congo to prepare the way for the more arduous task of building a responsible and viable Congolese government.

Even while UN troops were arriving in the Congo, further complications developed. Tribal antagonisms erupted into local wars; South Kasai, following the example of Katanga, seceded from the central government; and Moise Tshombe not only refused to dismiss his Belgian advisers and troops, but announced that he would meet with force any attempt by the United Nations to enter Katanga.

In the light of all these developments, Hammarskjöld thought it necessary in early August to return to the Council for a clarification of his mandate. The consensus between the superpowers continued to hold. Both the United States and the Soviet Union voted for a resolution sponsored by Tunisia and Ceylon which declared that "the entry of the United Nations Force into the province of Katanga [was] necessary," and demanded the immediate withdrawal of Belgian troops from the province.[4] The resolution was adopted by a vote of 9 to 0, with France and Italy abstaining. The United States voted for the resolution with some misgivings, because of the strong action against Belgium; the Soviet Union, which wanted even stronger action, had introduced a draft resolution that would have imposed upon the Secretary-General the obligation "to take decisive measures, without hesitating to use every means to that end," to remove the Belgian troops. But in the end, the Soviet Union too supported the Ceylon-Tunisia resolution.

Phase Two: The Breakdown of Consensus

The consensus between the superpowers broke down when, in the autumn of 1960, the new Congolese government disintegrated into factions. A power struggle between Premier Lumumba and President Kasavubu erupted. In September, the two leaders fired each other from their respective positions. In the melee, a young pro-Western colonel, Joseph Mobutu, took command of the armed forces. As a result, the position of the political leader most sympathetic to the USSR was undermined. Under Mobutu's rule, many Belgian administrators returned to the Congo as unofficial advisers.

The superpowers now took opposing positions on the two rival factions in the Congo government. The United States pressed the United Nations to recognize the Kasavubu-Mobutu government, while the Soviet Union began to support the deposed Lumumba with aircraft and trucks. The UN representative who was in charge of this critical phase of ONUC's operations in the summer and fall of 1960 was Andrew W. Cordier, Executive Assistant to Dag Hammarskjöld. Cordier's overriding concern was to uphold the Charter and to restore law and order in the war-torn Congo. In order to stop both Kasavubu and Lumumba from inflaming popular feelings even further and to prevent the outbreak of civil war, he decided to close all Congolese airports, to immobilize troops, and to shut down the national radio in Leopoldville. Three years later, Mr. N. T. Fedorenko, the Soviet delegate in the Administrative and Budgetary (Fifth) Committee of the General Assembly, was to declare that, by this action, "Cordier had adopted a decision that broke Lumumba's back" and had thus started the United Nations on its pro-Western course in the Congo.[5] Similarly, many highly placed U.S. officials later pointed to Cordier's decision as having "stopped the Russians." Cordier himself defended his action on the grounds that it had *not* been taken *against* one of the rival factions or *against* one of the superpowers, but *for* the law of the United Nations and the Charter.[6]

After the closure of airports and radio stations by the United Nations, the Soviet Union accused the United Nations of neocolonialism and proposed a draft resolution directing the United Nations to cease any interference in the internal affairs of the Congo and to hand over the airports and radio stations to the central government. Only Poland supported this resolution. Ceylon and Tunisia abstained and proposed a substitute resolution which endorsed the policies and actions of the Secretary-General. This resolution was vetoed by the Soviet Union.[7] The consensus between the superpowers had now broken down completely, paralyzing the Security Council. The General Assembly was immediately called into emergency session.

The superpowers now attempted to line up majorities for their

opposing positions in the General Assembly. The United States led
the forces seeking "to affirm and strengthen the mandate already
given to the Secretary-General by the Security Council." The Soviet Union, on the other hand, took the position that "the United
Nations Command and the Secretary-General personally have un-
masked themselves as supporters of the colonialists."[8] After intensive
and often acrimonious debate, an overwhelming majority of the
Assembly supported the Secretary-General's policy, appealed to
members to refrain from unilateral action in the Congo, and created a Conciliation Commission made up of African and Asian
representatives in order to pacify the internal dissensions in the
Congolese government.[9]

The General Assembly also considered another important matter
at this time: Who should represent the Congolese government in
that body? The Republic of the Congo had been admitted to
membership on September 20, but the question of seating its
representatives had been left to the Credentials Committee. Several
days later, Guinea proposed that, pending a decision of the Credentials Committee, representatives of the Lumumba government
should be seated. This proposal was supported by Ceylon, Ghana,
India, Indonesia, Mali, Morocco, and the United Arab Republic,
all of which had troops in the Congo. It was also vigorously defended by the Soviet Union.

The Guinean proposal brought a sharp protest from Kasavubu,
who immediately set out to plead his case at UN Headquarters in
New York. On November 8, he appeared on the rostrum of the
General Assembly and demanded the seating of his representatives.
He was supported in this demand by the United States, which
claimed that the Lumumba government did not have effective and
stable control of the country or the ability to fulfill its international
obligations. The Assembly debate was adjourned briefly, pending
the return from the Congo of the Conciliation Commission. But on
the Credentials Committee, which had been given a separate mandate after the vote of the Congo's membership, the West had a
clear majority. The United States proposed the accreditation of
the Kasavubu delegation, and after two days of heated debate the
motion was adopted in committee by a vote of 6 to 1. Lumumba's
supporters now had to bring their fight into the General Assembly.

Both superpowers lobbied intensively for their positions, especially among the African members of the Assembly. The United States was backed solidly by all the NATO powers, most of the Latin-American states, and a majority of the French-speaking African members, although a considerable number of African and Asian states which had endorsed the Congo policy of the Secretary-General now balked and either abstained or voted against it. The final vote on the critical accreditation issue was 53 in favor of seating the Kasavubu delegation, 24 opposed, and 19 abstentions. The United States position emerged victorious.

The Congo operation continued, but now it was clear that one of the superpowers no longer felt that it served its national interest. Though it could still be said that ONUC was impartially assisting the legitimate government of the Congo to restore order, it was obvious that the Soviet Union believed the Kasavubu government to be pro-Western. For this reason, the USSR vetoed the continuation of ONUC in the Security Council and, when the Secretary-General carried on the operation under Assembly authority, mounted the attack against him and his office discussed in Chapter 3. The United States, of course, insisted that it was supporting a disinterested UN operation that sought to restore peace and order in the Congo. One wonders, however, what American policy might have been had the Credentials Committee and the General Assembly seated Lumumba instead of Kasavubu.

Phase Three: The United Nations' Show of Force

On February 13, 1961, it was announced that Patrice Lumumba had been killed by hostile tribesmen in Katanga. This event, which convulsed the Congo and threatened to plunge it into civil war, led to a partial restoration of superpower consensus in the Security Council. On February 21, the Council, in a 9-to-0 vote with the Soviet Union and France abstaining, passed its strongest resolution to date, urging that "the United Nations take immediately all appropriate measures to prevent the occurrence of civil war in the Congo, including . . . the use of force, if necessary, in the last resort."[10] The resolution also called for "an immediate and impartial investigation" of Lumumba's death. The United States had some misgivings about the implications of the use of force, even "in the last resort," but the fact that most of the African and Asian states solidly supported the resolution helped persuade the American delegation to vote for it. The Soviet Union, also fearful of alienating the African states if it vetoed the "force in the last resort" resolution, abstained. Thus, with the reluctant approval of one of the superpowers and the tacit consent of the other, the Security Council—no longer veto-bound—resumed political direction of the Congo operation. The African states had thus been instrumental in restoring a partial consensus between the superpowers.

During the spring and summer of 1961, the Congo presented a picture of extreme confusion. Kasavubu had appointed Cyrille Adoula as Prime Minister of the Congolese government, but the Adoula government was unable to control the entire country. Lumumba's Vice-Premier, Antoine Gizenga, established the "legitimate government" of the Congo in Stanleyville. And ONUC forces, in their efforts to integrate Katanga into the central government, ran into mounting resistance, not only from the Katangese forces of Moise Tshombe, but from French, Belgian, and South African mercenaries. There were numerous casualties on all sides. Finally, on September 17, in an effort to persuade Tshombe to desist, the Secretary-General decided to go himself to Katanga, but was killed during a night flight when his airplane crashed near Ndola, in Northern Rhodesia. The tragic event imperiled the entire operation. Nevertheless, top officials in the UN Secretariat continued Hammarskjöld's work. On September 21, a provisional cease-fire was agreed upon, but ratification did not follow until five weeks later. The Security Council met on November 13, ten days after the election of U Thant as Acting Secretary-General. The continuing need to resolve the problem of Katanga resulted in an even stronger resolution than the one of February 21. With no negative votes and only France and the United Kingdom abstaining, ONUC was now authorized "to take vigorous action, including the use of the requisite measure of force for the immediate apprehension of all foreign military and para-military personnel and political advisers not under the United Nations command, and mercenaries."[11] Both superpowers strongly supported this antisecessionist resolution. The United Nations was now clearly committed to support Adoula's central government against the secessionist efforts of both Tshombe and Gizenga.

In early December, Acting Secretary-General U Thant directed UN forces to reestablish law and order in Elisabethville, the capital of Katanga. This initiative resulted in heavy fighting. The United Nations moved in heavy reinforcements for an all-out offensive to gain control in Katanga. But some Western powers, notably Belgium and Great Britain, still hesitated to see Tshombe suppressed. Apart from the considerable financial interest both countries had in Katanga, Tshombe was considered the only pro-Western anti-Communist, whereas Gizenga was seen as a serious Communist threat to the Congo, and the central government as being at best merely neutral. There were supporters of the Tshombe regime even in the United States. Britain refused to supply bombs to the United Nations to be used against Katanga. Some Western opinion viewed the danger of Communist influence as the greater threat, while the anticolonial African and Asian nations saw Tshombe as the tool of "imperialism," and therefore the major danger. The Soviet Union backed the anti-Tshombe forces.

The United Nations was now determined not to stop until the secession was ended. UN forces, supported by jet fighters, pressed on, and on December 20, Tshombe signed the Kitona Agreement, acknowledging the authority of the central government and promising to comply with the UN resolutions requesting the removal of foreign mercenaries. But talks to implement this agreement were not begun until March 1962, and in June, after a second breakdown of discussions, it appeared that Tshombe still had no intentions of ending his secession. In late July, U Thant submitted a plan for the reunification of the Congo, consisting of a 50-50 sharing of revenues from Katangese mines, integration of the Katangese army with that of the central government, and the discontinuance of separate representation abroad, in return for which Katanga would receive considerable local autonomy. U Thant intimated that if this plan was not accepted economic pressures would be used, possibly extending to a complete trade and financial boycott. But neither Belgium, Britain, nor the United States wanted pressures to go beyond the economic sphere, and Tshombe's conditional acceptance of the plan sufficed to avert any economic sanctions. In October, the West became preoccupied with the Cuban crisis and seemed content to let Congolese matters drag on. But the Chinese attack on India gave rise to Indian pressures to obtain the release of her troops in the Congo, numbering over 5,000 men, to fight in the Himalayas. Moreover, the weakening of Premier Adoula's position, occasioned by the central government's inability to enforce its authority in Katanga, created a need for the early settlement of the Katangese secession. Finally ONUC, which cost $120 million a year, was leading the United Nations into serious financial difficulties. These are discussed in the following chapter.

By December 1962, U Thant's plan to incorporate Katanga into the central government had not yet been carried out. Thus, the pressure for economic measures against Tshombe increased. Adoula had been requesting such measures since August, but at that time both Britain and Belgium had been opposed. Nor had the United States actively supported such a move. Now Belgium shifted its stand, in return for a promise from the central government to grant Katanga a large share of the mining revenue. The United States, too, threw its support behind Adoula. But Britain and the Union Miniere still refused to go along. Fighting again broke out in late December, but Elisabethville was captured by UN forces on December 28, and the important mining center of Jadotville fell a week later. At first it appeared that Tshombe was going to fight to the end and pursue a scorched earth policy which would ruin Katanga, but he surrendered his last stronghold at Kolwezi in return for a general amnesty for Katanga's officials. By the end of January 1963, the resistance was ended, but the situation continued tense throughout the rest of the year. In mid-1964, the last ONUC contingents were withdrawn from the Congo, and the problems of reconstruction and reconciliation among the many warring factions reverted to the Congolese government. Ironically, Moise Tshombe emerged as the new Premier of the Congo after the withdrawal of ONUC.

The only United Nations presence remaining in the Congo after June 1964 was the UN Civilian Operation. This undertaking had begun in July 1960 side by side with the UN's peace-keeping function. It aimed to keep intact transport and communications, sustain a decent level of public health, further education and public administration, and develop industry and agriculture. During the latter part of ONUC's work, the Civilian Operation became almost indistinguishable from a large and very ambitious technical-assistance program. Most of the Operation was financed from the UN Congo Fund. This Fund was supported by voluntary contributions from twenty governments. The United States at first contributed almost three-fourths and later about one-half of the expense. The remainder was paid by other Western countries. The Soviet Union made no contribution.

The problem of putting the Congo back on its feet politically and economically had been a staggering one. Indeed, maintaining ONUC in the Congo for four years had nearly bankrupted the United Nations. Like the King's men, the United Nations could not put the Congo back together again. But the presence of the Organization had at least brought a solution within reach. And it had prevented a major clash between the superpowers in the heart of Africa.

Conclusions

The Congo crisis, like the Suez crisis before it, may be seen in three concentric circles. It began as a local conflict among several warring factions or competing forms of nationalism. When the new Congolese government attacked the intervention of Belgium as an act of aggression, the tribal struggle merged into the larger one of nationalism versus colonialism. Finally, the superpower conflict entered the picture as the last and widest of the circles, with the Soviet Union gaining its first foothold in the Congo through Lumumba and the United States striving to oust the USSR by supporting the United Nations and Kasavubu.

The over-all record demonstrates that the two superpowers considered their national interests better served through UN action than through UN paralysis. The United States permitted the United Nations to act because it hoped to neutralize a "no man's land" in Africa from the East-West struggle and because it was impressed with the powerful African backing for UN action. The Soviet Union permitted the United Nations to act because it too wanted to woo the Africans in the United Nations and because a veto would have brought about immediate action in the Assembly, where the USSR had much less power and influence. Only when the Congo Operation began to go directly against the interests of one of the superpowers was a veto cast. And when the UN's policy became more acceptable, the Soviet Union once again stood clear.

Flexibility once again was a keynote. Political control of the Congo Operation passed from the Security Council to the General Assembly and the Secretary-General and finally reverted full circle to the Council. The Secretary-General had to adapt the Operation to a constantly changing UN mandate and to constantly changing attitudes not only on the part of the superpowers, but other key states in the Organization. When one considers that ONUC at various times was bitterly attacked by the USSR, opposed by France, and seriously questioned in influential quarters in Britain and the United States, one realizes that the Operation probably could not have survived without an extraordinary degree of adaptability to political developments. And, as in the Suez precedent, an additional element of flexibility characterized ONUC: the peace was kept not by activating the superpowers, but by carefully excluding them from the actual physical conduct of the Operation. It is true that ONUC had to be launched with the political support of both superpowers, yet it was able to survive against the will of one of them; and it was conducted without the troops of either.

SELECTED BIBLIOGRAPHY

Burns, Arthur Lee, and Nina Heathcote. *Peace-Keeping by UN Forces: From Suez to the Congo.* New York: Praeger, 1963.

Gordon, King. *UN in the Congo.* New York: Carnegie Endowment for International Peace, 1962.

Hoffmann, Stanley. "In Search of a Thread: The UN in the Congo Labyrinth," *International Organization* (Spring 1962), pp. 331-361.

"Issues before the Sixteenth General Assembly"; "Issues before the Seventeenth General Assembly"; "Issues before the Eighteenth

General Assembly," *International Conciliation*, Nos. 534, 539, and 544 respectively (September 1961, 1962, 1963).

James, Alan. *The Politics of Peace-Keeping.* New York: Frederick A. Praeger, 1969.

Lefever, Ernest W. *The Crisis in the Congo: A UN Force in Action.* Washington, D. C.: The Brookings Institution, 1965.

O'Brien, Conor Cruse. *To Katanga and Back.* New York: Simon and Schuster, 1963.

CHAPTER 6

The United Nations Financial Crisis and the Superpowers

The Western powers and their accomplices were alone responsible for the expenses occasioned by those illegal operations [UNEF and ONUC] which are now the cause of the United Nations' financial difficulties, and it is they that should bear those costs, so that the prestige of the United Nations might be maintained.

> Nikolai T. Fedorenko
> Soviet Delegate to the
> Fifth Committee,
> May 1963.

Mr. Chairman, there is a confrontation. There is a confrontation not between countries. There is a confrontation by the Soviet Union with the advisory opinion of the World Court. There is a confrontation of the Soviet Union with the acceptance of that opinion by the General Assembly. There is a confrontation by the Soviet Union with the solvency of the United Nations. In short, Mr. Chairman, there is a confrontation between the Soviet Union and the United Nations.

> Francis T. P. Plimpton
> United States Delegate to the
> Fifth Committee,
> May 1963.

While the United Nations was engaged in major peace-keeping responsibilities, there was never a shortage of Cassandras predicting that the Organization would end with a bang. However, during the height of the UN Operation in the Congo there existed a real possibility that it might have ended with a whimper. A fiscal crisis

developed in the early 1960's that became a threat to the life of
the Organization. The cause of this crisis was the refusal of the
Soviets and others to pay for the two operations that the United
Nations had mounted to keep the peace: the UN Emergency
Force in the Middle East (UNEF) and the UN Congo Force
(ONUC).

Never had so many people argued so much about so little
money. The financial crisis was in reality a political crisis over the
proper role for the United Nations to play in the national policies
of its member states, particularly the superpowers. Only secondar-
ily was it a crisis over the costs of UN membership.

The United Nations Emergency Force

As we have seen, the General Assembly authorized UNEF by a
vote of 64-0-12 in November 1956 and, after much delicate negotiation, over 6,000 men—contingents from ten countries (Brazil, Canada, Colombia, Denmark, Finland, India, Indonesia, Norway, Sweden, and Yugoslavia)—were ready for action. But it was
clear that unless the question of financing was solved, the Force
would not get beyond the paper stage. Hence the Secretary-General, in his proposals to the General Assembly, gave the matter
of financing the Force his most careful attention.

On November 21, 1956, the Secretary-General recommended
that a Special Account outside the regular budget be set up for
UNEF and that the costs of the Force be shared by the member
states on the basis of the scale of assessments to be adopted for
the 1957 budget. In addition, he suggested an initial appropriation
of $10 million to meet the immediate cash needs of the Force.

On December 3, the Secretary-General faced the problem of
allocating the balance of the expenses of the Force and indicated
to the Assembly that the only equitable way of meeting the costs
henceforth was to share them according to the 1957 scale of assessments. Although UNEF costs were financed under a Special
Account, the Secretary-General nevertheless considered them as
"United Nations expenditures within the general scope and intent
of Article 17 of the Charter."[1] Some states disagreed sharply with

this proposal, however, and it profoundly divided the Fifth Committee of the Assembly. The superpowers took opposing positions immediately.

The U.S. delegate agreed with the Secretary-General and pointed out that the Committee's decision would be of crucial importance for the future of the Organization. He was supported by most of the Western nations. This view was sharply challenged by the delegate from the Soviet bloc, who insisted that the entire cost of the Operation should be borne by those countries which had precipitated the crisis—Britain, France, and Israel.

Between these two opposing views, yet a third emerged: most of the smaller nations claimed that everyone should pay something, but that the Great Powers, which had special privileges under the Charter, should also shoulder special responsibilities and pick up the major portion of the bill.

This formula won the day in the General Assembly and was adopted by a vote of 62 in favor, 8 against, and 7 abstentions. Only the Soviet bloc voted against. Under the terms of the Resolution, everyone was expected to contribute, but nations with limited capacity to pay received rebates of up to 50 percent of their assessments. The United States pledged itself to make voluntary contributions in order to cover the deficits created by these rebates.

The decision to assess the member states by this "rebate formula" did not solve the problem of financing UNEF. The heart of the problem was how to collect the assessments. Each year, arrears and defaults amounted to roughly one-third of the total assessment. The largest single debtor was the Soviet Union, which justified its nonpayment with two arguments: first, that "the aggressors must pay" and, second, that UNEF was illegal in a fundamental sense, since only the Security Council had the right to authorize peace-keeping operations.

The Secretary-General's position was clear: all member states had a legal obligation to pay. This view was supported by a majority of the membership, and most adamantly by the United States.

Although the numerous arrears and defaults had put the United Nations into serious financial straits by 1960, UNEF never threat-

ened the financial structure of the Organization itself. It was the
Congo crisis which was to shake that structure to its very foundations.

The United Nations Congo Force

After the two superpowers had both voted for the authorization
of a peace force in the Congo in the Security Council on the
night of July 13–14, 1960, and a tenuous consensus had thus been
attained, the Secretary-General set about to put together and finance the new Force. On October 24, 1960, the Secretary-General
estimated the cost of the Congo Force for 1960 at $66,625,000.
Once again, he defended the principle of collective responsibility
as the most equitable method of sharing the financial burden. The
United States supported him, but the Soviet Union stated its intention not to contribute to any part of ONUC's expenses since,
in its opinion, "the main burden . . . should be borne by the chief
culprits—the Belgian colonizers."[2] The rest of the money should
be raised through voluntary contributions.

At this point, the Secretary-General presented his view to the
Fifth Committee. After strongly endorsing the principle of collective responsibility, Mr. Hammarskjöld deplored the tendency of
some delegations to approve courses of action for the United
Nations without following through financially:

> Will this organization face the economic consequences of its
> own actions and how will it be done? Further, if it is not
> willing to face the financial consequences of its own decisions,
> is it then prepared to change its substantive policies? There
> is no third alternative.

He then pointed up the resulting dilemma:

> The Secretariat finds itself in a difficult position. On the one
> hand, it has to pursue "vigorously" the policy decided upon
> by the General Assembly and the Security Council. On the
> other hand, it is continuously fighting against the financial
> difficulties with which these decisions under present circum-
> stances face the Organization. Of course, the Organization
> cannot have it both ways.[3]

Finally, the Fifth Committee, by a vote of 45 to 15, with 25 abstentions, approved a draft resolution proposed by Pakistan, Tunisia, and Senegal and supported by the United States. The resolution recommended an *ad hoc* account of $48.5 million for the expenses of ONUC, to be assessed on the basis of the 1960 scale; stressed that these assessments would be "binding legal obligations" on member states within the meaning of Article 17 of the Charter; called on the government of Belgium to make a substantial contribution; and recommended that voluntary contributions be applied to reduce by up to 50 percent the assessment of states with the least capacity to pay. On December 20, this recommendation was adopted by the General Assembly by a vote of 46 to 17, with 24 abstentions.

The second round was fought over the 1961 assessment of $100 million. Again, the Fifth Committee was deeply divided. Since the sum under consideration was the largest ever to be assessed by the United Nations for a single operation and since the decision would obviously have far-reaching consequences, more fundamental and elaborate arguments were raised by the superpowers than over the 1960 assessment. Moreover, the very solvency of the Organization depended on the outcome of the discussion. The United States once again favored the principle of collective responsibility on the basis of the 1960 assessment, although it offered to waive its reimbursement rights of over $10 million and to make a voluntary cash contribution of up to $4 million to be used to reduce the assessments of governments with limited capacity to pay.

The Soviet Union insisted that since ONUC was a Security Council "action" in the sense of Article 48 of the Charter, the General Assembly had no right to reach a decision on the matter. Article 11 of the Charter provided that any question involving peace and security on which action was necessary must be referred to the Security Council by the Assembly. Hence, in the Soviet view, ONUC financing should be governed not by Article 17 but by the unanimity principle in the Security Council. The Secretary-General stated in rebuttal that once the Security Council had taken a decision, the implementation costs fell clearly within the meaning of Article 17 and therefore within the bailiwick of the Assembly. The Soviet position, he argued, would have the effect of extending the unanimity principle of the Big Five to matters of finance, which would clearly lead to the paralysis of the entire operation in the Congo.[4]

Finally, the Fifth Committee adopted a draft resolution, originally sponsored by Ghana, Liberia, Pakistan, and Tunisia, and supported by the United States, which apportioned $100 million for the period January 1 to October 31, 1961, according to the 1960 assessment scale, "pending the establishment of a different scale of assessment" to defray ONUC's expenses.[5] This time reductions of up to 50 percent were granted the poorer nations in order to obtain the necessary two-thirds majority in the plenary Assembly. Voluntary contributions were to be applied to offset the resulting deficits. The Big Five and Belgium were called upon to make substantial voluntary contributions. The final vote, taken at dawn on the last day of the session, was 54 in favor, 15 against, with 23 abstentions. The Soviet bloc, Mexico, and Belgium cast negative votes, while France and South Africa abstained and subsequently refused to contribute.

The third round was fought in December 1961 over the 1962 ONUC budget. The Fifth Committee delegates went over much the same ground as in the previous debates and recommended an appropriation of $80 million to cover ONUC costs from November 1, 1961, to June 30, 1962. On December 20, 1961, the General Assembly, by a vote of 67 in favor, 13 against, with 16 abstentions, appropriated this amount, with the same provisions for reductions as were approved in April.

The only nation which made voluntary contributions in cash to the Congo Operation was the United States. The sums contributed between 1960 and 1962 totaled more than $30.6 million and were used to cover the deficits created through rebates given to the poorer nations.

At the time of the opening of the Sixteenth General Assembly in 1961, UNEF and ONUC arrears had brought the United Nations to the brink of bankruptcy. In the case of UNEF, forty-one members owed all or part of their assessments for the 1960 budget, bringing arrears to almost 25 percent, and sixty-five members owed all or part of their 1961 assessments, bringing the combined shortage to almost 30 percent of the total. In the case of ONUC, sixty-six members had accumulated a combined shortage of nearly 40 percent of the 1960 budget, and only twenty-four had paid their 1961 assessments.[6] The accumulated arrears for UNEF and ONUC by the end of 1961 exceeded $80 million, which was a sum larger than the annual regular budget. Two of the five permanent powers of the Security Council—the Soviet Union and France —had declared their intention not to make payment, and a third —Nationalist China—had defaulted.

As a result, the two peace-keeping operations had become heavily dependent on one of the two superpowers—the United States. Although the United States was assessed less than one-third of the 1961 UNEF budget, in effect, since its voluntary contribution was used to offset the reductions granted to fifty-one countries with limited capacity to pay, it was paying 43 percent of the total. In 1962, these reductions were increased and the United States assumed responsibility for a portion of the assessment of seventy-nine member states, which brought its share of the total cost to 48 percent. In the case of ONUC, the United States had assumed this larger share from the very beginning.

Such dependence on one superpower was not desirable, and, more important, the failure of other states to pay their assessments was reaching alarming proportions. The UN debt now exceeded $100 million. In April 1961, a Working Group of Fifteen was established which attempted to construct a special scale of assessment for peace-keeping operations. On November 15, 1961, this Working Group reported its findings to the Fifth Committee. In essence, the report was a catalogue of individual opinions largely retracing the ground that had been covered in earlier debates on UNEF and ONUC financing. Only one positive recommendation emerged from the discussions—a suggestion to ask the International Court for an advisory opinion on the applicability of Article 17 of the Charter to peace-keeping operations. In order to settle at least one argument in the financing controversy, the Assembly decided, on December 20, 1961, by a vote of 52 to 11, with 32 abstentions, to ask the International Court for an advisory opinion on the question: Did the expenditures authorized by the General Assembly for UNEF and ONUC constitute expenses of the organization within the meaning of Article 17 of the Charter?[7] Acting

Secretary-General U Thant also warned the Assembly at that time that the United Nations was faced with imminent insolvency if arrears and current assessments were not paid promptly. He estimated that, by June 30, 1962, the gap between the debts of the organization and its available net cash resources would exceed $100 million. Quite obviously, drastic emergency action was necessary to finance the peace-keeping operations beyond June 1962.

The Bond Issue:
The United Nations as Borrower

On December 20, 1961, the General Assembly also adopted Resolution 1739 authorizing the Secretary-General to issue bonds in the amount of $200 million. The Resolution provided that the bonds were to bear interest at 2 percent a year and that the principal was to be repaid in twenty-five annual installments by including in the regular budget each year beginning in 1963 an amount sufficient to pay installments of principal and interest charges. The bonds were to be offered to member states of the United Nations, members of the specialized agencies and of the International Atomic Energy Agency, and, if the Secretary-General with the concurrence of the Advisory Committee on Administrative and Budgetary Questions should so determine, to nonprofit institutions or associations. The sale of bonds was to continue until December 31, 1963.

The debate in the Fifth Committee which preceded the passage of Resolution 1739 was animated, and frequently heated. The superpowers took opposing positions. Strong support for the bond issue came from the delegates of the United States, Canada, Australia, Ireland, Ethiopia, Ghana, Ceylon, Burma, and the Netherlands. Philip M. Klutznick of the United States said that if all members paid their arrears on the peace-keeping operations, the Organization could forget about the proposal; but since the exact opposite seemed to be true, the Committee could not leave the Acting Secretary-General with a political mandate but without the means to carry it out. Any amount less than $200 million would be insufficient to put the UN house in order. The proposal was to be seen as a one-time emergency arrangement to keep the Organization alive. The opposition was led by A. A. Roschin of the Soviet Union, who declared that the deficit in the United Nations existed not because certain states failed to pay their contributions but because UNEF and ONUC were illegal under the Charter. A bond issue would make the United Nations a tool of the bond-holders. It was a maneuver to enable the United Nations to engage in similar illegal "peace-keeping" activities in the future.

The passage of the bond Resolution by the General Assembly was only the first step in securing the $200 million loan for the United Nations. In many member nations only legislative approval could authorize subscription to the bond issue. Most crucial, of course, was to be the decision of the Congress of the United States. When the U.S. delegate to the United Nations voted in favor of the bond Resolution, he stated at the time that only the Congress could authorize the purchase of such bonds and that his vote was to be considered as subject to this condition. Indeed, the fiercest legislative battle over the bond issue took place in the Congress of the United States.

On January 30, 1962, President Kennedy sent a special message to Congress to appropriate $100 million for the purchase of the bonds. Exhaustive hearings on the bill were held in the Senate Committee on Foreign Relations during February and March. The bond issue was defended by top-level members of the Administration, including Secretary of State Dean Rusk; Assistant Secretary of State for International Organization Affairs Harlan Cleveland; the United States Representative to the United Nations, Adlai Stevenson; and the United States Representative to the Economic and Social Council, Philip Klutznick. The merits of the bond plan were seriously questioned, however, by several members of the Committee on Foreign Relations, particularly Senators George D. Aiken (Republican, Vermont), and Bourke B. Hickenlooper (Republican, Iowa). These debates in the Committee were perhaps the most crucial phase in the history of the bond issue.

There were several strong arguments adduced in favor of the bond proposal. First, it was claimed that the bond issue would ensure the principle of collective responsibility, since the principal and interest payments on the bonds would come out of the regular budget, thus compelling nations to pay or risk the loss of voting privileges in the General Assembly. Second, it was asserted that the United States would save money in the long run, because, since the bonds would be paid back out of the regular budget over a twenty-five-year period, the United States would contribute to UNEF and ONUC operations on the basis of 32 percent instead of 48 percent as heretofore. Third, since the Secretary-General would be permitted to sell bonds not only to member states of the United Nations but also to members of specialized agencies and possibly to nonprofit institutions, the bond issue offered the prospect of new financial resources. Germany and Switzerland, for example, two nonmembers, would, it was hoped, purchase some of the bonds. Fourth, it was argued that the twenty-five years permitted for repayment would make each annual installment small enough for the burden on some of the smaller countries not to be unreasonable. Finally, the Administration defended the view that the bond proposal appeared to be the best temporary device for financing the two peace-keeping operations until a pay-as-you-go plan could be agreed upon. Moreover, the bond issue was not to be deemed a precedent for UN financing, nor was it intended to relieve nations in arrears of their responsibilities toward the two peace-keeping operations. The proceeds were expected to be large enough to carry UNEF and ONUC until the end of 1963.

While no member of the Committee proposed that the United States withhold emergency financial assistance from the United Nations, there was considerable concern about whether the bond technique was the wisest course of action. Senators Aiken and Hickenlooper suggested as an alternative that the United States should make a three-year loan of $100 million, with an annual interest rate of 3 percent, to help the United Nations over its financial emergency. The two Senators, who received considerable support in the Committee, questioned the bond device on a number of grounds. First, it was felt that, even though the bond issue was not to become a precedent, it would nevertheless encourage further fiscal irresponsibility by member states that were in arrears. Many might decide that if the United States bought one-half of the bonds, this amount would suffice and thereby relieve them of their own responsibilities. Hence, a short-term loan coupled with a vigorous attempt to collect arrears on past assessments would be preferable. The bond issue would simply postpone the moment of truth and encourage irresponsible nations to shift their burdens to others. Second, support for the bond issue in the General Assembly itself had not been overwhelming. While it was true that 58 nations had voted in favor of the bond resolution, 13 had voted against it, and 33 had abstained or had been absent, indicating that perhaps as many as 46 states did not support the bond proposal. Finally, it was feared that a bond issue would be merely a disguised form of assessment under which subscribing states would first pay up the arrears of delinquent states; then, when the bonds came due, the redemption money would come not from the states in arrears but from those which had both paid their assessments faithfully and subscribed to the bonds as well.

After weighing these conflicting considerations, the Committee on Foreign Relations, by an 8-to-7 vote, reported favorably on the bond bill. The alternative of a straight $100 million loan was narrowly rejected. The majority, however, decided to protect the United States by including the proviso that the President would be authorized to purchase $25 million worth of bonds without limitation, but that the purchase of additional bonds up to a total of $100 million would have to be matched by the aggregate amount purchased by other nations. Furthermore, in order to ensure repayment of the bonds, it was decided to deduct from the annual contributions of the United States to the regular budget amounts corresponding to principal and interest payments owed to the United States. Finally, it was made clear that the bond issue was not to set a pattern for the future financing of peacekeeping operations, but was to be regarded as an extraordinary one-time remedy for the financial ills of the United Nations.

The narrowness of the vote was a source of considerable anxiety to the Administration. It was feared that a hostile majority would develop on the floor of the Senate. Even if the bill did pass the Senate, passage in the House of Representatives was highly uncertain. Consequently, the White House supplanted the State Department as the intermediary with the Senate, in the hope of achieving an overwhelming Senate majority for the President's proposal. The result was agreement on a revised form of the bill; the money was to be designated as a loan but still made available for the purchase of UN bonds by the President at his discretion. This compromise, in which the President maintained the substance of his proposal and the Senators won their semantic point of designating the fund as a loan, produced a favorable vote on the Senate floor of 70 to 22. The bill as finally passed retained the original matching proviso as well as the condition that bond re-payments be deducted annually from the U.S. contribution to the regular budget. It also included a clause to the effect that the United States should use its best efforts to promote a pattern of UN financing that would make unnecessary any future large-scale borrowing.

The telling argument against a straight $100 million loan that finally won over the opposition was the fact that such a loan would certainly have precipitated a financial crisis after three years. It would have been like a pistol pointed at the head of the United Nations, since, in all likelihood, the world organization would have had no resources to repay the loan at the end of the three years. Moreover, the Senate shared the hope of the Administration that the bond plan would compel all members to pay their share of the costs of peace-keeping operations. The Aiken-Hickenlooper loan project would not have furthered the principle of collective responsibility. The battle in the U.S. Senate over the bond pro-posal was not solely, not perhaps even primarily, the result of a difference of opinion over the respective merits of a bond issue or a straight loan. The bond controversy became a catalyst and brought into the open a good deal of doubt, suspicion, and am-bivalence about the United Nations as a whole. The role of the United Nations in Katanga, the rising power of the African and Asian nations in the General Assembly, and the increasing intran-sigence of the Soviet position—all these stimulated a broad reas-sessment of the world organization. The difficulties which the bond proposal experienced in the U.S. Senate were largely to be ex-plained in terms of a genuine and serious questioning of the role of the United Nations—especially its peace-keeping function—in the foreign policy of the United States.

The battle in the House of Representatives was no less intense. In September 1962, that body, by a vote of 256 to 134, settled on a bill which permitted the United States merely to match bond purchases of other UN members up to $100 million. The Senate version would have permitted outright U.S. purchase of $25 million. In the last analysis, the more restrictive version was adopted by the Congress. Hence, the full $200 million worth of bonds authorized by U Thant could be raised only if members other than the United States should buy $100 million.

By late 1965, sixty-five states had subscribed to the bond issue, many of them subject to legislative approval. The total amount purchased had reached almost $150 million, of which the United States had bought almost $75 million. Only in the United States had the condition of legislative approval posed a serious threat. Everywhere else, parliaments approved the pledges of their delegations with relative ease.

Superpower Showdown

It had always been clear to even the strongest supporters of the bond issue that the measure would have to be regarded as a stop-gap emergency device pending a permanent solution of the problem of financing peace-keeping operations. One ray of hope appeared when, on July 20, 1962, the World Court declared in a 9-to-5 Advisory Opinion that the costs of UNEF and ONUC were to be considered as legally binding obligations upon the entire membership. The Seventeenth General Assembly, on December 19, 1962, after a debate which covered familiar ground, decided to "accept" the Advisory Opinion by a vote of 76 in favor, 17 against, and 8 abstentions. As a result, a considerable number of smaller nations cleared their accounts, but the Soviet Union and France refused to abide by the opinion. Since France was paying for UNEF, it became increasingly obvious to all concerned that the first major nation to fall under the penalty provisions of Article 19 would be the Soviet Union. Under the terms of this Article, member states delinquent in their assessed contributions for two years or more could lose their votes in the General Assembly unless that body specifically waived the penalty.

In the meantime, the General Assembly reestablished the Working Group and increased its membership from 15 to 21. The enlarged Working Group continued to search for a solution to the impasse. The Soviet-bloc countries stuck to their contention that only the Security Council had the right to impose assessments for peace-keeping operations. The United States stiffened its position and declared its opposition to any special scale of assessments for UNEF and ONUC for the last six months of 1963 which would involve an assessment percentage for the United States in excess of 32.02 percent. The new U.S. position was based on the assumption that the regular scale made ample adjustments for low per capita-income countries and the belief that the financing of UNEF and ONUC for the last six months of 1963 should be handled on an *ad hoc* basis by methods which would not necessarily constitute a pattern for the future.

The bond money was virtually exhausted by early 1963. Hence, the Assembly had to meet in emergency session in May 1963. It assessed $42.5 million for the two peace forces for the last six months of 1963 according to the regular scale, with a 55 percent reduction to the developing countries. In December, it appropriated $17.75 million for UNEF for 1964, but decided to allot only $15 million to carry ONUC through June 1964.

While conditions in the Congo had improved somewhat, the Assembly's action was taken with at least one eye on its own problems. The accumulated Soviet debts for UNEF and ONUC were rapidly reaching the point at which the USSR would run the risk of losing its vote in the General Assembly under Article 19 of the Charter. The Assembly had no desire to precipitate a major political and constitutional crisis at a time when its military and financial problems in the Congo were still considerable. It was hoped that, after the Congo operation was concluded, some compromise might be arranged concerning the Soviet payments and that the Article 19 crisis could be avoided. Thus, the Assembly was in an increasingly conservative mood and the combined cash appropriations for UNEF and ONUC for 1964 amounted to less than one-fourth of those appropriated for 1963.

The threat of a constitutional and political crisis over Article 19 had another and, perhaps in the long run, more important impact upon the Assembly than reducing the appropriations for ONUC in late 1963 and 1964. New threats to the peace arose in

1962 in West New Guinea, in 1963 in Yemen, and in 1964 in Cyprus, and the United Nations had to make some provisions to meet its responsibilities. In West New Guinea, the United Nations established the UN Temporary Executive Authority (UNTEA) and arranged to have the costs shared jointly by the Netherlands and Indonesia. Similarly, in 1963, the expenses of a UN Observer Group in Yemen were split between Saudi Arabia and Egypt without cost to the United Nations. The expenses of the UN peace-keeping force in Cyprus were met by voluntary contributions every three months. In September 1964, Secretary-General U Thant had a hard time raising the modest sum of $7 million needed to keep the 6,400 man force in Cyprus for another three-month period. The original motive behind the move to split the costs between the involved nations in UNTEA and in Yemen was probably to spare the United Nations additional financial strain at this critical juncture and to try to wrap up the Congo operation *before* Article 19 fell on the Soviets, in the hope that the latter would make some sort of voluntary payment once the operation was over. In these three cases, however, the United Nations took an important step away from the collective responsibility principle upon which it had insisted previously. In two cases it was only the "involved" countries that paid. In Cyprus the voluntary contributions further underscored the disintegration of the collective responsibility principle. In sum, in an effort to postpone a showdown on this principle, the United Nations, with United States support, created three precedents that undermined it.

By 1964, even the Secretary-General admitted that "if the UN does not settle its past, it may not have much of a future." In June 1964 the last UN troops left the Congo, and the operation to which the USSR had been so much opposed was thus brought to an end. It was now hoped that some compromise could be reached on the Soviet debt. The usual September opening of the General Assembly was postponed until December 1 in order to give diplomats an opportunity to work behind the scenes. The United States, unsure of the support of the Afro-Asian countries and fearful of a showdown, decided not to fight the issue on its merits and would have agreed to a voluntary, unspecified Soviet payment sufficiently large to escape the sanction of Article 19. The United States and other members proposed numerous face-saving compromises to the USSR which would permit that country to make a payment without yielding its basic position that the peace-keeping operations were illegal violations of the Charter. However, no compromise was reached and as December 1 approached, positions hardened. The United States took the stand that the penalty should go into effect automatically and was determined to enforce it against the Soviet Union if the latter withheld payment. The USSR, on the other hand, insisted that a decision to suspend a member from voting could be obtained only by a two-thirds vote of the members present and voting. It based its case on Article 18 of the Charter which requires a two-thirds majority for Assembly decisions on "important" issues, including "the suspension of the rights and privileges of membership." A week before opening day, the United States declared that it would withhold pledges to the Special Fund until the Soviet Union paid enough of its arrears to avoid the application of Article 19, and the latter stated that, if it were stripped of its voting rights, it would leave the United Nations.

In order to avoid a head-on collision between the superpowers, the Secretary-General proposed on opening day that the Assembly conduct its business on a "no objection" basis, that is, without taking formal votes until some compromise on the debt issue could be hammered out. This proposal was accepted and established an uneasy truce between the superpowers during which further possibilities for compromise could be explored. The Afro-Asian nations proposed a "rescue fund" to which all members, including those in arrears on their peace-keeping assessments, would make voluntary contributions. After protracted and laborious negotiations, the Soviet Union committed itself to the Secretary-General to pledge an unspecified voluntary contribution, but refused to name the amount and date of payment, demanding in return that the Assembly resume normal business and voting procedure. The United States refused to accept this proposal, describing it as a "pig in the poke." In effect, the Soviet Union demanded the right to vote now and pay later, while the United States insisted that the Soviet Union pay first and vote later.

In the meantime, the tenuous "no vote" procedure threatened to break down when a sharp disagreement arose over one of four nonpermanent Security Council seats to be filled by December 31, 1964. While three candidates were unopposed, the fourth seat was hotly contested by Jordan and Mali. Since neither candidate was prepared to yield, the President of the Assembly, Mr. Alex Quaison-Sackey, proposed a special "consultation" procedure which, in effect, was tantamount to voting, with the single difference that the location of the ballot box was outside the Assembly hall. When three of these "straw polls" failed to break the deadlock, the two candidates reluctantly agreed to split the term.

New Year's Day of 1965 added France and ten other states to the list of members that were in danger of losing their voting rights under Article 19. Thus the crisis assumed more serious proportions, since, by now, over 10 percent of the membership, including two great powers, fell under Article 19. The "no vote" procedure continued, but under it none of the important agenda items could be touched. Shortly before the Assembly was to adjourn, the delegate of Albania threatened the precarious superpower truce by demanding an immediate resumption of normal voting procedure. The Assembly, however, in an overwhelming vote of 97 to 2, with 13 abstentions, overruled the Albanian demand, both superpowers voting with the majority. The United States, in a tactical retreat, permitted this one vote, declaring that it was merely procedural and thus did not compromise the American position on Article 19. On February 18, the General Assembly adjourned until September 1, 1965, with the main problem—the issue of Article 19—as far from solution as ever.

The Nineteenth General Assembly had thus managed to avoid an open confrontation between the superpowers over the application of Article 19. The Afro-Asian group had tried desperately to find some middle ground and had succeeded in making modest headway. The Soviet Union did offer to pledge a voluntary contribution, though it refused to name the amount and date of payment under "American blackmail." And the United States had to look on while the Soviet delegate cast his "vote" in the "consultation" over the seating of Jordan and Mali on the Security Council and had to permit a General Assembly vote to continue the "no vote" procedure.

As the Nineteenth General Assembly adjourned, a curious situation prevailed. The superpowers continued to be at odds with each other over the issue of Article 19. But the Afro-Asians were becoming increasingly frustrated with the superpowers since no important UN business could be transacted on a "no vote" basis. Hence, by early 1965, the confrontation between the two superpowers on the one hand and almost everyone else on the other had become almost as important as the U.S.–Soviet confrontation itself. The financial crisis had become a mirror of a significant political fact: the United States and the Soviet Union, if they chose to, could still virtually paralyze the more than one hundred other member states of the General Assembly. But finally, and perhaps most important, almost the entire membership *including* the superpowers made a common front against one member, Albania, which —probably prompted by Communist China—tried to precipitate a showdown that neither superpower wanted. Hence, there emerged a partial community of interest between the superpowers which made both of them rally to the defense of the United Nations itself.

What was basically at stake in the tug of war during the Nineteenth General Assembly was the principle of collective responsibility. The USSR opposed it and the United States chose not to fight for it on its merits. While the USSR's opposition was understandable, the problem of the United States was far more complex. On the one hand, the United States had a clear commitment to the principle; its support of the UNEF and ONUC financing patterns and its approval of the World Court Advisory Opinion left little doubt on that score. On the other hand, from a tactical point of view, the United States feared that it would lose a showdown vote or, if it won, that the victory might be indecisive or even Pyrrhic. The Afro-Asians were most eager to avoid a confrontation and were deeply divided on the merits of the American position. Second, there was the nagging fear that the collective responsibility principle might not always be congruent with the U.S. national interest in the future. Indeed, the right to pick and choose the peace-keeping operations one supported might one day be to the advantage of the United States. These conflicting considerations led to the ambivalence that characterized the U.S. position.

Finally, shortly before the opening of the Twentieth General Assembly, the United States gave up the fight over Article 19. On

August 16, 1965, Ambassador Arthur J. Goldberg announced that "the United States regretfully accepted the simple and inescapable fact of life that a majority of the 114 member states was unready to apply Article 19." Thus it now became unlikely that the United Nations would soon again venture into massive peace-keeping operations against the will of a superpower. It seemed, instead, that future operations would have to be based on a broader political consensus and be more modest in scale. It also seemed that the financial counterpart of collective responsibility, the assessment principle, would be superseded, at least temporarily, by that of voluntarism. The United Nations would require a period during which past gains would have to be consolidated before new advances could be made.

Conclusions

The financial crisis of the United Nations has aroused acute anxiety among many observers, who see it as the unmistakable symptom of an early death of the Organization. They point to the history of the League of Nations, maintaining that, in its case, financial atrophy was the first harbinger of doom, and claim that the same omens are now gathering over the United Nations: the penury of states and the Organization's mounting deficits.

On closer scrutiny, this analogy does not hold up. Many of the symptoms are similar, to be sure, but the root causes are quite different. The fiscal plight of the League had been the symptom of a struggle over its very existence. Many states had questioned the *raison d'être* of the League; others had tolerated it; certainly very few states wanted it to move beyond the concept of a "static conference machinery." In that sense, the League's chronic financial anemia had been the result of a struggle between nihilists and conservatives: those who would deny its existence altogether and those who would relegate it to the peripheries of their national policies. The former attitude had led to active hostility; the latter to political neglect and indifference.

The UN's financial plight is not the expression of a struggle over the Organization's existence. All states, including the Soviet Union, have accepted its presence. The struggle has moved onto a higher plane. It is now being waged between the conservatives and the liberals: those who wish to maintain the United Nations as a "static conference machinery," and those who wish to endow it with increasing strength and executive authority. Viewed in this light, the financial crisis of the United Nations does not indicate that the Organization has fallen into political collapse, but rather that the membership has not yet been willing to ratify and sustain its rise to a higher plane of development.

If one examines the superpowers' attitude in detail, it is clear that the "liberal" and "conservative" labels must be used with caution in the areas of peace-keeping and financing. It is true that the United States has generally favored the creation of peace-keeping machinery as a collective responsibility of the membership, whereas the USSR has tended to reject the assessment principle for UN peace forces. But as we look at specific cases, it is clear that the Soviet Union has not always said "no" with equal vigor. In fact, until 1963 the Soviet Union paid for a considerable number of minor peace-keeping operations that were financed through the regular budget. It acquiesced in the establishment of UNEF and actually voted for the creation of the Congo Force and only later tried to destroy it. Finally, and under great pressure, it came close to offering a payment toward UNEF and ONUC costs, although ostensibly as an unspecified and general contribution to the United Nations. Hence, the Soviet attitude has varied and can be portrayed in terms of a spectrum ranging from acquiescence through passive resistance to active obstruction. Moreover, these attitudes often changed during one operation. The changing Soviet position toward the Congo Force is a case in point.

Similarly, the states favoring UN peace-keeping operations do not always say "yes" with the same degree of enthusiasm. Some states, like the United States, support the political resolutions authorizing the establishment of the peace forces, then vote for the financing resolutions and make payment as well. Others have second thoughts at the second stage and abstain or even vote against the financing resolutions. And some that vote "yes" in the first two stages finally refuse to make payment after all. The liberal position on peace-keeping forces also extends along a fluid continuum: enthusiastic support, moral support, and tacit consent. The more cautious form of liberalism and the permissive form of conservatism often meet in voting terms, if not in principle, on the common ground of abstention.

Thus, both "liberals" and "conservatives" have varied their position over a broad spectrum. In fact, most states have responded to specific peace-keeping cases in terms of national interest rather than abstract principle. This is particularly true of the superpowers. From the U.S. point of view UNEF and ONUC sealed off a "no man's land" in the cold war from a possible East-West military confrontation and reduced the likelihood of unilateral intervention by the Soviet Union. The Soviet Union could reason that UNEF and ONUC prevented Soviet bridgeheads in the Middle East and Africa. Since, in the latter case, a bridgehead had already been established and had to be liquidated under UN pressure, Soviet opposition to ONUC may have taken a more active form. Thus, the financial crisis over UNEF and ONUC was really a political crisis over the proper role and control over these forces. The Soviet Union did not oppose UNEF and ONUC because it did not want to pay for them; it did not want to pay for them because it opposed them.

No one knows how the United States would react to a UN peace-keeping operation that conflicted with its national interests, because to date the United States has never been on the wrong end of a UN police action. In part, this fact is due to good luck. If Kasavubu had been killed in the Congo instead of Lumumba, the ONUC operation might have provided an interesting test of the American commitment to the principle of collective responsibility in the financing of peace-keeping operations. American voting supremacy in the United Nations, described in Part I, has also been important in preventing issues like the 1954 coup in Guatemala from being considered at any length by the United Nations. What the United States would do in a minority position against a UN operation is difficult to estimate, but, as we shall see in Part III, the United States has not hesitated to attack UN operations contrary to its national interest in the far less sensitive economic and social areas of the Organization's work. The point here is not to indict the policies of the superpowers, but to suggest that in peace-keeping matters it is misleading to associate the United States or the Soviet Union too closely with any philosophical position toward the United Nations in the abstract. Each case is decided in accordance with the national interest as it arises.

While the positions of the superpowers have had little to do with finances per se, in the case of many of the middle and smaller powers a weak financial position and the relatively large sums involved have played a far larger, and in some instances even a decisive, role. It is a fact, for example, that in terms of percentages of their gross national products twenty-one nations are called upon to make larger contributions to total UN costs than the United States. Hence, while the financial crisis of UNEF and ONUC was caused primarily by the political conservatism of the few, it was deepened by the financial limitations of the many.

The toughest problem, therefore, is that of coming to grips with the politically motivated deficits. One way to face up to the challenge completely would be to construct a scale which permitted a member to refuse payment for a peace-keeping operation it opposed. Such a solution would ignore the message of the Advisory Opinion that *all* member states should pay and would instead squarely confront the political reality that no power, certainly no great power, can be coerced into payment. It is also important to make a distinction between passive and active opposition. If opposition remains limited to nonpayment as was the Soviet Union's opposition to UNEF, supporters may wish to override it, provided they are ready to pay the share of the recalcitrant power. But if they override active opposition, they may drive the obstructionist power out of the United Nations altogether unless they are reasonably sure that the opposition will revert to a milder form, as the USSR's did in the Congo. The central truth that emerges is that the launching of an operation in the face of either passive or active opposition by a major power is in fact to ask for a financial crisis, and any state which asks for such a crisis may have to be prepared to bail the Organization out. At the heart of this problem is the stark fact of international life that no power, least of all a super-power, will adopt or easily acquiesce in paying for a policy which it considers inimical to its national interest.

SELECTED BIBLIOGRAPHY

Gross, Leo. "The International Court of Justice and Peace-Keeping Expenses of the UN," *International Organization* (Winter 1963).

Jackson, John H. "The Legal Framework for United Nations Financing: Peace-Keeping and Penury," *California Law Review* (March 1963).

Singer, J. David. *Financing International Organizations.* The Hague: Nijhoff, 1961.

Stegena, James A. *The United Nations Cyprus Force.* Columbus: Ohio State University Press, 1968.

Stoessinger, John G. "Financing the United Nations," *International Conciliation,* No. 535 (November 1961).

————, and Associates. *Financing the United Nations System.* Washington, D.C.: The Brookings Institution, 1964.

U.S. Senate, *Purchase of United Nations Bonds.* Hearing before the Committee on Foreign Relations, 87th Congress, 2nd Session, 1962.

PART III

The Superpowers and United Nations Economic and Social Operations

CHAPTER 7

Human Rights: The International Refugee Organization

There are human values which transcend states and governments.

United States Delegate to the
UN General Assembly,
January 1946.

The highest value to which a human being can aspire is to have a homeland, to be part of a sovereign state.

Ukrainian Delegate to the UN
General Assembly, January 1946.

While peace and security operations have often been improvised crash programs, social and economic activities have generally been stable, long-range, and steadily growing commitments of the United Nations. There has been little opposition to them in principle. The political issue in this realm has not been whether these programs should exist, but how quickly and by how much they should be expanded.

This concluding section examines the interaction of the superpowers in the field of UN economic and social affairs. One hope motivating the UN's participation in this kind of work was expressed by David Mitrany in *A Working Peace System* in 1946. He argued that the bonds of international order might be forged more rapidly by first concentrating on specific common problems in the less sensitive spheres of economic and social affairs. It was hoped that such activities could be isolated from political controversy and that habits of collaboration thus developed between the superpowers might gradually be extended into the strife-torn areas of political and even military security. The chapters in this section examine three different areas of economic and social activity: refugees, atoms for peace, and technical assistance. The actions of the superpowers in these areas provide three case studies testing the validity of Mitrany's functionalist thesis.

The Refugee Problem

The end of World War II found millions of people rendered homeless and destitute, as if a crazed giant had scattered the seeds of future unrest. Through the combined efforts of the Allied armies and the UN Relief and Rehabilitation Administration (UNRRA), eight million of these displaced people were repatriated to their former homelands. But about one million *refused* to be repatriated. Of these, Poles formed the largest group—roughly two-thirds; the remainder were composed of Balts, Yugoslavs, Ukrainians, Spanish Loyalists, and Jews. Dispersed though they were through many refugee camps in the Western zones of Germany and Austria, these uprooted people were as one in their refusal to return to countries where a dictatorship was in power.

The controversy over what should be done with this "last million" refugees led to the establishment of one of the most ambitious, massive, and costly operations ever undertaken by the United Nations—the International Refugee Organization (IRO). The negotiations that led to the creation of the IRO are among the most arduous on record in the United Nations. In essence, they turned on three fundamental questions: first, did these one million people constitute an international problem? second, were they to be permitted to choose freely between going home or resettling elsewhere? and third, what, if any, international assistance should be given those who would choose not to return?

Although most member states were involved in the discussions, the main protagonists were the two superpowers. In the course of debating the fate of these one million people, the two great powers touched on fundamental questions of human liberty. Their differing concepts of justice and mercy emerged with pristine clarity. Their views of man's relationship to the state stood out in stark and vivid contrast. Finally, the negotiations marked the transition between the hopes for a brave new world of postwar collaboration and the chilling reality of the cold war. That fateful first session of the UN General Assembly in 1946 intensified the somber contours of U.S.–Soviet relations in the years to come.

The International Character of the Refugee Problem

The question of refugees and displaced persons appeared as Item 17 on the agenda of the First Session of the General Assembly. This item attracted little immediate attention and was referred to the Third Committee of the General Assembly, concerned with social, humanitarian, and cultural questions.

The first issue that confronted the delegates was the dimension of the refugee problem. At an informal meeting of the Western powers in New York City in September 1945, the United States had proposed that some kind of international organization would be necessary to cope with the problem of the "last million" refugees. It was agreed that, since repatriation had dwindled to a trickle, it could no longer be regarded as a solution; the primary task of the projected organization would have to be the permanent resettlement of these unrepatriables. Some international authority would be best equipped for such a task.

In accordance with this view, P. J. Noel-Baker, delegate of the United Kingdom, proposed at the first meeting of the Committee that "there might be created, under the United Nations, under the direct authority of the Assembly, an organ of the United Nations which would take over the responsibility of the existing bodies."[1] Mrs. Eleanor Roosevelt, delegate of the United States, after agreeing with Mr. Noel-Baker, emphasized the necessity of establishing an international organization to come to the aid of the refugees in order to restore social equilibrium throughout the world. A. A. Arutiunian of the Soviet Union, supported by the Yugoslav delegation, challenged this contention and proposed that "the most practical way to solve this problem of Displaced Persons is by bilateral agreement between the two countries concerned—the country of origin and the country of refuge."[2] The Soviet position did not men-tion the possibility of resettlement. Implicit in the suggestion of bilateral negotiation between the country of refuge and that of origin was the liquidation of the refugee problem through repatriation.

At this juncture, the press began to pay attention to the proceedings in the Third Committee. The lack of agreement was described as an "ominous portent" by the *London Times.* The *New York Times,* in an editorial, sharply reminded the delegates that "this involves the fate and status of hundreds of thousands of human beings who are clearly an international responsibility. Unless UNO develops this human side of cooperation . . . it will labor in vain to lay the foundations for peace."[3] It was M. R. Knowles, the delegate from Canada, who brought some incisive logic to bear on the apparent deadlock. "If there is a problem," he asserted,

> . . . the proposal put forward by the United Kingdom will make it possible to find out what the problem is and to decide what should be done about it. On the other hand, if the United Kingdom proposal is adopted and it is discovered that the Yugoslav contention is correct, that there is no problem, no harm will have been done . . . if the Yugoslav proposal is adopted, it seems to me that, in effect, it closes the door.[4]

The strength of this argument prevailed and resulted in the unanimous acceptance by the Committee of the international character of the problem.[5] Of course, Soviet acquiescence on this issue did not weaken its position with regard to the future role of the international organization. In this respect, the concession by the USSR was largely a tactical one.

The "Priority Resolution"

The issue now confronting the Third Committee was how the refugee problem could most equitably and speedily be settled. Mr. Arutiunian from the Soviet Union struck the keynote when he asked, "What does every refugee expect from the organizations of the United Nations? . . . He expects help to be able to return to his native country."[6]

This view was supported by Dr. Bebler of Yugoslavia, who declared in effect that the only Yugoslavs outside the borders of his

country refusing to be repatriated must by definition be war criminals, quislings, and traitors.[7] He pointed to the examples of the
Ustashis, Zborachis, and the Chetniks as pro-Fascist elements who
should be made to face justice at home without delay. His conclusions from these observations were logical enough.

> Has it ever been known in the history of international rela-
> tions that a Government contributed to the cost of maintain-
> ing its political enemies who have fled abroad or—a fortiori
> —emigrants who have in fact committed crimes against the
> people? No, nothing of the sort has ever been known.[8]

While the United States recognized that there might be war criminals among the displaced persons, it felt that this was no justification for a denial of free choice to the refugee group as a whole.
As Mrs. Eleanor Roosevelt put it: "A refugee should be given
freedom of choice between repatriation or resettlement in a new
home. My Government cannot support a policy of compulsory repatriation."[9] This view was backed by all the Western delegates on
the Committee.

Thus, the outlines of the two positions began to assume form
and substance. The superpowers were in agreement on the international character of the refugee problem, but a sharp cleavage
emerged regarding the nature of operations to be assigned to the
new organization. The United States and the other Western countries felt that political dissidence was a legitimate phenomenon.
Since voluntary repatriation to the countries of origin had practically reached a standstill, the logical task of the new organ would
be the resettlement and permanent reestablishment of the remaining refugees. The Soviet position did not admit the existence of
bona fide refugees not wishing to return. Such persons were *ipso
facto* traitorous and reprehensible. The only just course would therefore be speedy repatriation and retribution. As for genuine refugees,
none would hesitate to return home, where they would be received
with open arms.

In its broad implications, the American position defended the
right of the individual to differ politically from his government.
The Soviet Union denied that right and considered it a punishable
offense. The United States visualized the new organization pri-

marily as a service organ for the reestablishment of the political dissident in a more friendly environment, while in the minds of the delegates from the USSR the proposed refugee organ was to oversee the repatriation process regardless of individual preferences. The United States insisted that the alternative of repatriation must remain a voluntary one, whereas the Eastern governments repeatedly stated and continuously implied the principle of enforced repatriation of all their dissident nationals. The West's conception of the United Nations in this instance was that of a service organ for the benefit of *individuals*, whereas the East saw it as a service organ for the attainment of the political aims of *states*.

The superpower deadlock was temporarily broken by P. R. Belehradek, delegate from Czechoslovakia, who suggested that, after all, no hard and fast delineation between repatriation and reestablishment would be necessary. The Committee, he proposed, should strive at a compromise solution, by voicing its collective preference in terms of a priority.[10] This suggestion was welcomed by the harassed Committee. The Soviet delegate admitted that two exceptions to his general principle certainly were in order: The Polish Jews could not be expected to remain in Germany and Austria, nor should they be compelled to return to Poland, where a renewed wave of anti-Semitic sentiment was on the upgrade. Similarly, the Spanish Loyalist refugees in France should not be compelled to return to Franco's Spain. Other solutions would have to be found for those two groups.[11] Most of the delegates, including the United States, agreed with this assertion, and the proposal of the Czechoslovak delegation was unanimously adopted.

The Committee did not deliberate long on the nature of the priority. It was agreed by all delegates that repatriation would be preferable to migration for a refugee in a foreign country. Such a solution, as long as it remained a voluntary one, would eliminate the inevitable difficulties a refugee would have to face in a new environment, and also would involve much less expense for the new organization. The wording of the Committee's resolution was left vague enough to be a general statement of policy only: "the [new refugee organization's] main task concerning displaced persons [is] to encourage and assist in every way possible their early return to their countries of origin."[12]

Once the Committee had unanimously agreed that repatriation of a voluntary nature was preferable to reestablishment, ways of effectuating that decision had to be explored. It was noted that most of the refugees were concentrated in camps scattered throughout Germany, Austria, and Italy, making it comparatively easy to adopt a unified policy for the operation of all these camps. It was at this point that a report from UNRRA reached the Committee revealing that repatriation of refugees to their countries of origin had been diminishing steadily to a negligible monthly total.[13] Various reasons were given in the report to explain this trend, the most important being the repugnance the average refugee felt toward his homeland as a result of his sufferings there, as well as his increasing disinclination to return to countries where regimes feared by the refugee had come to power.

The Ration Bribe

The Soviet Union now attempted to use material assistance to refugees as a political weapon to induce repatriation. It proposed that all repatriates should be supplied with food rations to cover a period of about three months.[14] The French delegate suggested that such assistance should not be reserved to repatriates, but should be made equally available to refugees seeking reestablishment elsewhere.[15] Mr. Arutiunian countered that, in view of the destruction evident in the countries of origin, repatriates certainly should be given preferential treatment. He was supported in this opinion by Sir George Rendel of the United Kingdom.[16] Mrs. Roosevelt disagreed: "No premium should be given to anyone to return to his country of origin. Six and a half million have returned without such a premium."[17]

Mrs. Roosevelt's implication that the food ration was a form of bribery was undoubtedly justified. The Soviet-bloc countries found themselves desperately short of manpower needed to rebuild their devastated areas. An inducement of a three months' ration supply might well make up a refugee's mind to decide in favor of repatriation. Mrs. Roosevelt asserted that reestablishment would, in effect, mean a much more difficult process of initial adjustment for the refugee and would therefore be deserving of at least equal material assistance.[18] The Damocles sword of bankruptcy was raised over the proposed organization by the delegate of the United Kingdom, who reminded the Committee that it would be a financial impossibility to supply every refugee with pecuniary aid. Only the most desperate cases could be considered.[19] Immediately, the Ukrainian delegate contended that, since the main task of the organization, as had been resolved, would be "to assist and encourage in every possible way the early repatriation of refugees to their countries of origin," obviously such material assistance would fall within the framework of the adopted resolution. Since the means at the disposal of the projected organ would be extremely limited, he continued, only repatriates should be supplied with rations.[20]

The logic of this strategy was hard to defeat and the implications of the "Priority Resolution" became increasingly clear to the dismayed delegates defending assistance to resettlers. The budgetary limitation was absolute. A choice had to be made, since none of the delegates proposed the huge additional expense implied in the French and American suggestions. On the other hand, there was no move in favor of reducing the three months' supply of rations per capita in order to increase the coverage. The delegates agreed reluctantly that a three months' ration supply should be given to all refugees and displaced persons choosing to be repatriated.[21]

The seriousness of this decision was not at first apparent. Although the Soviet bloc had not succeeded in pushing through a resolution embracing the principle of enforced repatriation, the new provision constituted in fact a form of bribery, offering an inducement to repatriation. It denied, in effect, a form of international assistance to one group of refugees while granting it to another, thus imposing a penalty upon freedom of choice. Considered in perspective, the decision constituted a tactical victory for the Soviet Union. It was the last issue in the IRO debate on which unanimity prevailed.

End of Compromise:
The Issue of Individual Freedom

At the opening of the ninth session of the Committee on February 8, 1946, the Soviet and Yugoslav delegates submitted the following resolution for adoption by the Committee: "No propaganda should be permitted in refugee camps against the interests of the Organization of the United Nations or her members, nor propaganda against returning to their native countries."[22] The proposal was accompanied by a vitriolic attack on the UNRRA administration of several dozen refugee camps in Germany, Austria, and Italy. The Soviet delegate contended that "camp personnel indulge in physical pressure to prevent refugees from choosing repatriation. Blows and beatings are freely resorted to to dissuade those who wish to return to their former homes."[23]

On the next day, the Committee received a communication from UNRRA headquarters signed by Herbert H. Lehman, director-general.[24] In it Mr. Lehman stated that, to his knowledge, twenty-two of the thirty camps cited in the indictment did not exist at all. As for the others, the director-general continued, it was the administration's policy to exert no pressure on camp inmates, but rather to encourage an independent and intelligent decision based on information regarding the conditions of life in the refugees' countries of origin. Such information was being regularly distributed by UNRRA authorities.

The Soviet-Yugoslav statement was thus discredited before the Committee. The USSR, however, insisted on a consideration of the proposal by the assembled delegates, since it rested squarely upon the premise of the "Priority Resolution." "Repatriation should be encouraged and assisted in every way possible," the Soviet delegate reiterated. Consequently, propaganda discouraging refugees from returning should not be tolerated in any refugee assembly center. Mrs. Roosevelt succinctly showed the Committee the dangerous implications of the proposed resolution: "Who is to decide what is propaganda? We are here to encourage as much individual freedom as possible. We shall do nothing to restrict individual liberty."[25]

Mr. Arutiunian countered sarcastically that it was not the business of the Committee to encourage war criminals, quislings, and traitors to disseminate their propaganda in refugee camps. "We are being entirely too tolerant," he exclaimed. "But such tolerance is the tolerance of Munich. It is, in fact, appeasement which must lead, in the final analysis, to serious international repercussions."[26] Mrs. Roosevelt then posed the following question to the assembled delegates: "Are we of the United Nations so feeble that we have to forbid human beings to voice their thoughts; are we so weak that we have to fear their discussion with their friends?"[27] The spirit of her late husband pervaded the chamber when she added, "We should not exaggerate our fears and begin to be afraid of fear itself."[28]

At this crucial moment, Mme. N. M. Lefoucheux, delegate of France, stepped into the breach, offering the following resolution:

> No refugees or displaced persons who have finally and definitely, in complete freedom, and after receiving full knowledge of the facts including adequate information from the government of their countries of origin, expressed valid objections to returning to their countries of origin, and who do not fall in the category of war criminals, quislings, and traitors, shall be compelled to return to their country of origin.[29]

The principle of voluntary repatriation was implicit in the French proposal. Since this was already incorporated in the "Priority Resolution," that particular aspect was not discussed. The ensuing discussions turned on the two points involving the dissemination of information in the refugee assembly centers. The debates focused on the two phrases "adequate information" and "valid objections." Mrs. Roosevelt, strongly supporting the French resolution, insisted on the broadest possible definition of "adequate information." Only a painstaking and conscientious observance of the principles of freedom of speech would ensure freedom of choice for the refugee —the only desirable solution. As for "valid objections," Mrs. Roosevelt defined such objections as including political dissidence from the governments in power in the countries of origin.[30]

Mr. Arutiunian of the Soviet Union countered in reply that, since most of the refugees were nationals of Eastern nations, it was only fair to give the Eastern governments precedence in the matter of information. The French and American definition of "valid objections," he continued, "would invite the protection and escape from punishment of elements hostile to the United Nations."[31] He then suggested that the Committee should constitute itself as a Commission of Enquiry in order to determine the eligibility of refugees expressing "valid objections" to their return.

The delegates of the United States and Panama defended the majority view. "The refugee must be allowed to make up his own mind and must be given the tools to do so."[32] The other Western delegates, although admitting that some reprehensible elements could no doubt be found among the refugees, agreed that such persons would certainly be in the minority. It was not the wish of the Western nations to help undesirables escape from justice. But the large majority of refugees should not be allowed to suffer because of a few such persons.

The Soviet position remained adamant; a similar rigidity was by now characteristic of the United States and the Western powers. Further debate was fruitless and, since unanimity was impossible, the Western powers pressed to settle the issue by a vote, which showed a clear division between East and West on the issue of free speech in refugee camps. The French resolution was passed by the Committee by a vote of 13 to 5, with 3 abstentions.[33]

The vote was the first instance of a majority decision in the Committee, all previous issues having been settled by unanimous decision. This fact was noted with regret by the chairman. The *New York Times* greeted this event somewhat more joyfully in an editorial entitled "Free Speech Wins Out in UNO Refugee Committee."[34] *Pravda*, on the other hand, decried bitterly the "betrayal of United Nations principles and protection of quislings, war criminals, and traitors by the capitalist Powers." Furthermore, the Soviet organ continued,

> One is tempted to believe that those nations who defend so ardently the right of refugees to emigrate to new countries of resettlement want to profit from the occasion through the acquisition of cheap labor. Recently, American papers have expressed the opinion that it would be advisable to take in 20,000 refugee women as domestics.[35]

The rigidity of the Soviet stand was not surprising. Neither the Soviet Union nor the other countries of origin were anxious to lose the manpower implied in refugee resettlement, nor could they be expected to look benignly upon an organization responsible for relocating approximately a million people who had rejected Communism as their form of government. On the other hand, the Western traditions of freedom of speech and the right of political asylum were too deeply entrenched to be dismissed lightly. No international organization comprising the major Western powers could be expected to operate on any other principle. The ultimate cleavage was a reflection of the competing ideologies emerging on the international scene.

The Soviet Union now attempted a different approach to attain a measure of control over the international organization to be established for dealing with the refugee problem. A new resolution was proposed by Mr. Arutiunian. It stipulated that "the personnel of refugee camps should be comprised mainly of representatives of states concerned, whose citizens are the refugees."[36] The Polish delegate, Mr. Stanczyk, supported the Soviet proposal by pointing out that, since most of the refugees were nationals of the Eastern countries, a staff composed mostly of nationals of the countries of origin would be best qualified to deal with them.

The implications of the Soviet draft resolution were immediately apparent to the members of the Committee. Such a resolution, if adopted, would place all refugee camps under the administration, and therefore policy, of the Soviet bloc. The Western powers, therefore, were adamant in their rejection of this principle. As one spokesman pointed out: "The proposal is almost frightening. The idea that refugees who are opposed to the governments of the countries of origin should be placed under the authority of those whom they fear cannot be considered even for a moment."[37] The Soviet draft resolution was defeated by the same division as prevailed on the previous vote.

Shortly before the Committee was scheduled to adjourn, the Soviet bloc made one further attempt to obtain control over refugee camp operations. The Yugoslav delegate made the following proposal:

> Those refugees who are not war criminals, quislings, or traitors and who do not wish to return to their countries of

origin, should receive assistance in their early settlement in a
new place with the consent of the governments concerned—
that of the country of their origin and the country of resettlement.[38]

The last phrase was the key, however, and would have given a veto
power to the countries of origin on the question of giving or withholding resettlement grants to their nationals. The resolution was
defeated by the same vote as before.

The lines of battle between the superpowers had been clearly
drawn in the Third Committee debate. It was now time to turn
from discussion of principles to the concrete task of drafting a
constitution for the IRO. The General Assembly established a Special Committee on Refugees under the auspices of the Economic
and Social Council. This Committee decided to establish a nonpermanent specialized agency of the United Nations to deal with
the refugee problem with a first-year "rock bottom" budget of
$193,954,000. In addition, an administrative budget of $4,800,000
and a special resettlement fund of $5,000,000 were also set up.
Since the total number of eligible refugees was estimated at
1,391,000, this budget provided a daily per capita expense of
roughly forty cents per refugee. It was to be financed by a mixture
of assessment and voluntary contributions from the members.[39]

The fruits of this labor came up for final consideration at the
Second Session of the General Assembly in December 1946. Mrs.
Roosevelt delivered the most impressive address for the West. She
hailed the IRO Constitution as "an expression of the high ideals
and aspirations for which the United Nations stands," urging its
signature and ratification on all member governments. However, the
Soviet delegate had the final word, asserting that "we have tried
to correct the Constitution with a series of amendments, but since
they have been rejected, we consider the Constitution to be un-
satisfactory."[40]

The dramatic final vote came on December 15, 1946. It showed
29 member nations in favor of the Constitution and 5 against, with
18 abstentions.[41] A clear bifurcation between the superpowers was
evident.

Conclusions

A year of labor had finally produced the IRO. An analysis of the
events throughout the year shows that the initial flexibility on the
part of the superpowers gradually disappeared. The early sessions
of the Third Committee were conducted on the unanimity principle, but as the superpowers' radically different conceptions of a
"refugee" emerged, this harmony was shattered. In the end, the
West, led by the United States, used majority diplomacy to establish
its position, first in the Third Committee and later in the General
Assembly.

The USSR's denial of such freedom was obviously rooted in its
basic attitude toward dissident elements. By definition, all dissidents
were traitors and should be treated accordingly by their home
governments. Enforced repatriation would have ensured that. In
order to rebuild the Eastern countries after the vast devastation
resulting from the Nazi occupation, a large reservoir of manpower
was needed, to which the repatriated displaced persons would contribute. Furthermore, the refusal of a million people to live under
Communism was a major political setback. To the Soviet point of
view, these national-interest considerations were the overriding ones.

The West was really asking the Communist countries to join and
contribute to an organization that would assist in the resettlement
of people who had rejected their governments. By analogy, the
question may be raised whether the United States would have
agreed to join and support an international body that would resettle American citizens who did not wish to return to the United
States. Perhaps the Soviet Union would have joined the IRO had
it been asked to make financial contributions to the maintenance
and repatriation, but not to the resettlement, of the refugees. But
such a proposal was never made.

The American position was doubtless rooted in the strong tradition of the right of asylum and freedom of speech and assembly,
and dictated by a liberal conception of the scope of individual
liberty and freedom of choice. However, this moral stand also co-
incided with the national interest of the United States. The spec-
tacle of over one million refugees "voting with their feet" against
Communism would certainly tarnish the Soviet image in Europe.

In sum, as the cold war deepened during 1946, the United States was very conscious of the political implications of the refugee problem as well as of its moral and humanitarian aspects.

While national-interest objectives remained firm on both sides, tactics were flexible. We can observe a steady progression in tactics on each side until the basically antithetical national interests were fully revealed. Thus, the USSR's first objective was to turn the IRO into a repatriation agency; when that failed, it sought to obtain control over the refugee camps and then to have a veto over the refugees' resettlement plans. When all these tactics were blocked, the Soviet Union boycotted the organization. The United States, on the other hand, had the voting power to ensure its interests. At first, it tried to work through the unanimity principle and made some compromises, such as the "ration bribe," in order to keep the Soviet Union within the framework of the system. But soon it had to call for majority votes; and finally, it ended up with an all-Western organization over which it had complete control.

The final result of the debates leading to the establishment of the IRO was a somewhat paradoxical one. The influence of the Soviet Union on the new organization was manifest despite its refusal to become an active participant. The emphasis on repatriation as a preferable mode of settlement, reinforced by the "ration bribe," which was in the main unsuccessful in attracting repatriates, certainly stemmed from Soviet considerations of its national interest.

The repudiation of the new organization by the Russians was a mixed blessing. It did allow the IRO to function more efficiently, owing to the basic agreement on fundamental considerations among the participating states. On the other hand, the universal character of the organization was sacrificed. Thus, in Mitrany's functionalist terms, the creation of the IRO was not a success. The debates over refugees, instead of drawing the superpowers closer together, had pushed them further apart. Since most of the people involved were refugees from Communism, this was hardly surprising. The refugee issue was itself too intensely political to lend itself easily to the Mitrany approach.

In the final analysis, however, the fundamental clash over human rights between the superpowers did not result in general paralysis. The founding of the IRO signified an about-face with respect to the refugee problem by at least a part of the world community. For the first time in history sovereign nation-states made a determined effort to come to the defense of the homeless and the destitute. By its firm leadership, the United States probably saved hundreds of thousands of innocent human beings from a tragic fate in forced-labor camps behind the Iron Curtain. The IRO was the first great attempt to approach the refugee problem on a global scale.

SELECTED BIBLIOGRAPHY

Claude, Inis L., Jr. *National Minorities.* Cambridge, Mass.: Harvard University Press, 1955.

Holborn, Louise W. *The International Refugee Organization.* New York: Oxford University Press, 1956.

Lauterpacht, H. *International Law and Human Rights.* New York: Praeger, 1950.

Mitrany, David. *A Working Peace System.* Chicago: The Quadrangle Press, 1966.

Penrose, E. F. "Negotiating on Refugees and Displaced Persons," in Raymond Dennett and Joseph E. Johnson, eds., *Negotiating with the Russians,* pp. 139-68. Boston: World Peace Foundation, 1951.

Read, James M. "The United Nations and Refugees—Changing Concepts," *International Conciliation,* No. 537 (March 1962).

Stoessinger, John G. *The Refugee and the World Community.* Minneapolis: University of Minnesota Press, 1956.

—— • ◄ • ► • ——

CHAPTER 8

The International Atomic Energy Agency and the Nonproliferation Treaty

The United States pledges before you—and therefore before the world—its determination to help solve the fearful atomic dilemma—to devote its entire heart and mind to find the way by which the miraculous inventiveness of man shall not be dedicated to his death, but consecrated to his life.
                                    Dwight D. Eisenhower
                                    UN General Assembly,
                                    December 8, 1953.

The level of science and technique which has been reached at the present time makes it possible for the very application of atomic energy for peaceful purposes to be utilized for increasing the production of atomic weapons.
                                    Vyacheslav Molotov
                                    Soviet Foreign Minister
                                    April 1954.

The hopes for the International Refugee Organization failed in one sense, because one of the superpowers refused to join. A decade later, both superpowers helped to create, and joined, a new member of the UN family—the International Atomic Energy Agency. A comparison of the two cases casts some revealing light on the superpowers' policies in the economic and social activities of the United Nations.

The Proposal

When President Dwight D. Eisenhower first launched the idea of the International Atomic Energy Agency in his address "Atomic Power for Peace" delivered before the United Nations General Assembly on December 8, 1953, he stated that "The United States would be more than willing . . . to take up with others 'principally involved' the development of plans whereby peaceful use of atomic energy could be expedited."[1] The President further stated that, "of those 'principally involved,' the Soviet Union must, of course, be one."[2]

The United States first proposed a statute for the projected agency in a Department of State memorandum handed to Soviet Ambassador Zarubin on March 19, 1954.[3] During the following five months five similar memorandums followed. All were rejected by the USSR, the last one on September 23, 1954. These early outlines contained many features of the Agency Statute to be adopted two years later by eighty-two states, including the Soviet Union.[4] The USSR at first rejected the entire idea of an Atoms for Peace Agency, claiming that the American plan evaded the important issue, the control of nuclear weapons, and would tend to intensify the atomic armament race.[5] The Soviet government, during the first six months of diplomatic correspondence with the United States, stressed that the issues of disarmament and the peaceful uses of atomic energy were inseperable. Mr. Molotov's solution to the dilemma was a restatement of the Soviet position on the disarmament problem: prohibition of nuclear weapons would have to precede the creation of the Atoms for Peace Agency.[6] The United States maintained that the two issues could be separated:

> In reality, ways can be devised to safeguard against diversion of materials from power producing reactors. And there are forms of peaceful utilization in which no question of weapon grade material arises.[7]

The mid-1954 deadlock reflected in many aspects the struggle between the superpowers over disarmament. According to the Soviet government, the prohibition of nuclear weapons would have to precede any constructive consideration of the problems of atomic energy, including the proposed Atoms for Peace Agency. In the American view, effective international control of nuclear weapons would have to precede prohibition.

At this juncture the United States decided to proceed with the negotiation of a draft statute without the Soviet Union. Ambassador Morehead Patterson, representative of the U.S. Department of State, issued invitations to seven other "atomic powers." Delegations from Australia, Belgium, Canada, France, Portugal, the Union of South Africa, and the United Kingdom met in Washington in the summer of 1954. The U.S. government stated again that it kept the door open for the Soviet Union to join the group. At the outset, however, it appeared as if the IAEA, like the IRO, might not have the membership of one superpower.[8]

Superpower Coordination: Negotiating the Statute

On September 22, 1954, in a dramatic about-face, the Soviet Union indicated its willingness to separate the issues of disarmament and peaceful uses of atomic energy and to accept the eight-power draft as a basis for further negotiations.[9] The USSR served its national interest in several ways by joining the negotiations on the proposed Agency. By participating in the drafting of the Statute, the Soviet Union could prevent the Agency from taking on the aspect of a hostile alliance and becoming an exclusively Western club with a membership closely resembling NATO's. Soviet absence from the Agency would have identified the United States as the leading nation in the scientific and technological development of nuclear energy for peaceful purposes. Most important, the Soviet could oppose the Western atomic powers in the name of the atomic "have-nots," the underdeveloped countries. By raising the specter of "atomic colonialism," the Soviet Union could expand its role as self-appointed champion of the oppressed and the exploited.

When the question of the Agency was first discussed in the Ninth General Assembly's First Committee in the fall of 1954, the Soviet delegation expressed consternation at the small size of the group that was to set up the Agency. It was composed "exclusively of

European and quasi-European powers."[10] Henry Cabot Lodge, now on the defensive, countered by stating that the American government would invite

> All governments to submit their views to Washington for serious consideration. The document would not be presented to the Assembly as a *fait accompli*. But the Assembly [was] not the appropriate place to draft the Agency Statute—a long and complex document.[11]

Mr. Menon, delegate of India, answered that

> The General Assembly is precisely the place for drafting the Statute. All nations should have an equal part in the actual elaboration of the Agency.[12]

As a result of these criticisms and the pressure of the General Assembly, the U.S. government, on July 29, 1955, decided to make the draft Statute the subject of multilateral negotiations. First, Brazil, Czechoslovakia, India, and the USSR would be invited to join the original eight sponsors and, second, the completed new twelve-power draft would be submitted to all members of the United Nations and its specialized agencies at a conference on the final text of the Statute.[13] Thus, after this opening round, the superpowers were already in opposing corners.

The twelve-power negotiations in Washington, from February 27 to April 18, 1956, were the crucial stage in the evolution of the Statute. During these six weeks a delicately balanced compromise document emerged which received the unanimous support of the drafting powers. A study of the negotiations reveals an interesting relationship between the superpowers. They had a joint interest as atomic-producer powers that gave them a closer understanding with each other on certain issues than with the atomic have-nots.

The Statute negotiators decided that the Agency was to have three organs: a Board of Governors, a General Conference, and an administrative staff headed by a Director-General. But the nature and composition of each of these organs as well as the relationship among them presented stubborn problems.

The thorniest issue was the composition of the Board of Governors. This organ was to be given preponderant authority "to make most of the necessary decisions for the Agency since the membership as a whole [could not] deal with day-to-day technical problems."[14] At first, the Soviet Union and the United States were in accord on this issue and visualized an atomic parallel to the UN Security Council. The top atomic powers—the United States, the Soviet Union, the United Kingdom, France, and Canada— would be given permanent seats and special voting privileges. Five other powers were to be selected on a rotating basis from the other principal producers and contributors of source materials. Six countries were to be elected to the Board by the entire membership of the Agency through the General Conference.[15]

The principle of an "Atomic Security Council" with five permanent powers was sharply criticized as undemocratic by Mr. Bhabha, India's delegate, who spoke generally for the large majority of atomic have-nots. At this point, the Soviet Union abandoned its position with the atomic haves and assumed its role as anticolonial spokesman. It supported the Indian position by stating that

> The Board of Governors must have adequate representation of all parts of the world. A large Board is necessary since it will perform world-wide functions. The current figure of sixteen members proposed by the United States is insufficient.[16]

The United States continued to insist on a small Board in which the atomic powers should have a privileged and permanent position.

The final solution was a delicately balanced compromise resulting in a cumbersome Board of twenty-three members. First, the top five atomic powers—the United States, the Soviet Union, Canada, France, and the United Kingdom—were given what amounted to permanent membership as long as they retained their leading positions in the atomic energy field in their respective geographic areas—North America, Western Europe, and Eastern Europe. It was not stipulated who would decide—and how—the retention of their status as leading atomic powers. Second, the top atomic power in each of the remaining five geographic areas was to be designated a member of the Board through co-option by the permanent members.[17] Brazil, South Africa, Australia, India, and

Japan were placed into this category. Third, two producers of source materials were to be designated on an annual rotating basis from the following four countries: Belgium, Czechoslovakia, Poland, and Portugal. Czechoslovakia and Portugal were designated to the first Board. Fourth, one nation would be designated on an annual rotating basis as a supplier of technical assistance. On the first Board this role was given to Sweden. Finally, to meet the demands of the atomic have-nots, six members of the Board would be annually elected by the entire membership of the Agency through the General Conference.[18]

A unique mixture of self-perpetuation, co-option, and election thus emerged from the twelve-power discussions on the membership of the Board of Governors. When the formula was brought up for debate at the Statute Conference in September 1956, it was once more bitterly attacked by the underdeveloped countries as an "atomic club formula." A series of amendments were proposed, recommending that the elected members of the Board be equal to the number of those designated.[19] The Soviet Union now rejoined the United States in defense of the twelve-power draft:

> The draft article before the Committee seems to be a reasonable compromise. In a spirit of cooperation the delegation of the Soviet Union has decided not to move any amendments . . . and hopes that the same spirit of cooperation will prevail among other delegations. . . .[20]

Mr. Wadsworth, U.S. representative, thanked the Soviet delegate for his support and added that the formula "[represented] a finely balanced compromise even a small part of which [could] not be changed without affecting the whole."[21] Mr. Bhabha, the Indian representative and spokesman for the have-nots, now admitted that "the formula [had] been arrived at by give and take on all sides."[22]

The evolution of the Board was therefore a record of compromise between the atomic powers and the atomic have-nots. The Soviet Union alone varied its position. Originally, it sided with the haves and then, during the twelve-power discussions, it defended the interests of the have-nots. Finally, it aligned itself with the haves again during the Statute Conference.

Serious cleavages also marked the negotiations determining the powers of the General Conference in relation to the Board of Governors. The Soviet Union aligned itself with the atomic have-nots, demanding a more powerful role for the General Conference. It proposed that the number of Board members elected by the General Conference be increased from six to fifteen.[23]

The American delegation restated the arguments used in its defense of the Board's composition and added that since the Agency would be an operational organization its executive arm should be given as much independence as possible.[24]

Once more several concessions had to be made, all of which increased the power of the General Conference. First, the number of elected Board members was raised to ten. Second, it was agreed that, if the Board was unable to arrive at a decision on a matter which it would then choose to refer to the General Conference, the latter body would have not only the power of recommendation but also the authority to "take decisions."[25] Finally, the twelve-power draft gave the General Conference the authority to "discuss any questions or any matters within the scope of the Statute. . . . and [to] make recommendations to the membership of the Agency or to the Board of Governors or to both on any such questions or matters."[26] This provision was considered to be a powerful instrument of pressure on the Board, patterned after Article 10 of the UN Charter enlarging the powers of the UN General Assembly. In fact, this increase in the powers of the General Conference, as the negotiations progressed, was reminiscent of the early negotiations on the powers of the United Nations. At San Francisco, the authority of the General Assembly was considerably increased as a result of pressure from smaller states, in contrast to the original Dumbarton Oaks proposals that had emphasized the functions of the Security Council.[27] These concessions proved sufficient to have the new twelve-power draft endorsed by the Statute Conference.

A similar tug of war broke out during the discussions on the role of the Director-General, the chief administrative officer of the Agency. The USSR and India took the position that, once appointed, the Director-General should be equally responsible to the Board and the General Conference. The delegates from the United States and the United Kingdom countered with the following argument:

It is unsound and quite impracticable to make a senior official responsible to two bodies. It is not really fair or wise to ask any man to serve two masters. Once appointed, the Director-General should be responsible to the authority which is ultimately responsible for the conduct of the Agency's operations —the Board of Governors.[28]

At the Statute Conference this view convinced those delegates who felt that sound administrative principles had to overrule mistrust of the atomic powers on the Board. The Soviet Union again associated itself with those Afro-Asian countries which remained unconvinced. At the final vote, however, the Anglo-American position prevailed by a large majority.

Both superpowers had expressed concern over the problem of safeguards to prevent the diversion of atomic materials to military uses soon after President Eisenhower's 1953 address in the General Assembly, but their solutions differed radically. The Soviet Union claimed that safeguards were meaningless and that only a complete ban on atomic weapons would solve the problem. The United States advocated rigorous and foolproof safeguards, but rejected an uninspected ban on nuclear weapons.

The Soviet Union broke this deadlock in 1954 when it agreed to join the twelve-power group. It accepted the principle of safeguards but expressed concern about the infringement on recipient nations' sovereignties through its operation.[29] India, however, in the twelve-power group voiced adamant objections to the American proposal to establish an international inspection system, stating that this would set up a double standard under which only non-atomic states would have to undergo inspection. The USSR, while supporting the concept of safeguards "in principle," actually threw its support behind the Indian position in practice. The United States, however, continued to insist on a rigorous system of safeguards against diversion.

Finally, the following specific safeguard powers were written into the Agency Statute: First, the Agency would have the right to examine the design of any nuclear reactor before it was built in order to determine whether it complied with Agency regulations. The Agency would withhold approval of a design which would make diversion of materials difficult to detect. Second, the Agency would be empowered to require the maintenance of operating records. Third, the Agency would reserve for itself the right to approve the chemical processing of radioactive material not usable for peaceful purposes. Hence, stringent controls were to be exercised over those key points in the processing where diversion to weapons could most readily take place. Finally, the Statute established a system of inspection through a staff of international inspectors.[30] In essence, the compromise formula retained the key elements of the American position.

The adoption of the principle of inspection by international civil servants was without precedent. The powers seemed much more concerned with the matters to be inspected than with the principle of inspection per se, although the Soviet Union kept reminding the delegates that "this function of the Agency was to be carried out with due observance of the sovereign rights of recipient nations."[31]

When the Agency Statute was unanimously adopted by the International Conference in October 1956, it closed a unique series of negotiations between the superpowers. In the discussions about the Agency's structure and the controversial problem of safeguards, the conflicts between the superpowers were sometimes less divisive than those between the atomic and nonatomic powers. In the dispute over the Board of Governors, the USSR sided primarily with the atomic powers, led by the United States. On the questions of the power of the General Conference and the responsibilities of the Director-General, the Soviet Union supported the anticolonial powers, although occasionally offering some compromises. The USSR supported the American position on safeguards "in principle" and the opposing anticolonial powers' position in practice, but in the end it threw its weight behind a compromise that, in fact, gave the Agency inspection powers at key points where military diversion could take place.

The Soviet Union's ambivalent behavior throughout the negotiations gives some indication of the uncomfortable position in which it was caught. Its national interest as an atomic power dictated that the new Agency be responsibly controlled and, particularly, that atoms given for peace should not contribute to the dispersion of atomic weapons for war. On the other hand, the

Soviet national interest also called for support of the anticolonial nations in their efforts to prevent the creation of an Agency which, in their view, would impose on them a kind of atomic neocolonialism. The USSR's dilemma in this instance was analogous to that of the United States when that superpower was caught between the demands of its Western allies in NATO, on the one hand, and those of the new anticolonial nations, on the other.

In the case of the United States, its common interest with the Soviet Union as an atomic producer power injected a high degree of harmony into its relations with the USSR in the twelve-power discussions. While the United States also sought friends in the underdeveloped world, it saw its national interest better served by an agency modeled along the lines of its original proposal rather than one that would make numerous concessions to the demands of the have-nots. As it was, the disagreements with India and other representatives from nonatomic countries were more intense than those with the Soviet Union.

Superpower Conflict: The Agency in Action

In its early negotiations, the Board of Governors strenuously attempted to maintain the unanimity principle in its decision-making process, even in highly controversial matters. For example, the nomination of Mr. Sterling Cole, an American, for the post of Director-General, was severely criticized by the USSR, which wanted a chief executive from one of the neutral powers.[32] Nevertheless, the Soviet delegation chose not to vote against Mr. Cole's appointment. As the subject matter discussed by the Board became increasingly controversial, the Board gradually dropped its attempts at unanimity. At least three schisms—at times appearing simultaneously—tended to make the Board a house divided. The superpowers frequently adopted opposing positions that had to be brought to a vote for a decision. The problem of inviting a representative from the European Atomic Energy Community (Euratom) to the Second General Conference was a case in point. The Soviet delegation maintained that "no argument could cancel the military character of Euratom. Inviting an observer would set a dangerous precedent."[33] The delegate of the United States, supported by the majority of the Board membership, defended Euratom's participation, since "the Community [Euratom] was not only devoted to the peaceful uses of atomic energy, but was destined to become a powerful force in that field."[34] No compromise was possible or even attempted. By a vote of 15-3, with 5 abstentions, the Board decided to issue the invitation.

The Board was also split between the atomic powers and the underdeveloped countries. The Soviet Union, once again caught between its conflicting roles as atomic producer and self-appointed benefactor of the anticolonial powers, often resolved this dilemma by abstaining from voting. The problem of planning for the building of reactors was an example. The atomic powers contended that most of the world's underdeveloped regions—for a variety of reasons—were ill-prepared for immediate erection of reactors. The have-nots, on the other hand, reminded the Board of the Statute's injunction to "make provision . . . for materials . . . and facilities . . . including the production of electric power, with due consideration for the needs of the underdeveloped areas of the world."[35] A majority of the Board, the Soviets abstaining, decided to limit the Agency's preliminary activities in this area to the creation of fact-finding teams to determine the needs and absorptive capacities of the underdeveloped countries. Again, it was impossible to attain unanimity.

The third division on the Board followed no particular international lines. It concerned fiscal policy. The Board has been extremely conservative on matters of finance. The American delegation was the only one defending a generous fiscal policy, but it was consistently outvoted. The issue of establishing research facilities at Agency Headquarters was one case among many. The American delegation felt that laboratory research at Agency Headquarters would lead to "invaluable services to the underdeveloped countries."[36] The Soviet delegate defended the view that such research should be conducted in the underdeveloped countries by visiting experts. Any Agency research laboratory was considered premature and "might cost the peoples of member states countless millions of dollars."[37] The Soviet view was supported by a majority of the Board membership, including the United Kingdom and Canada.

Another case of superpower friction over fiscal policy involved the Division of Safeguards. The USSR held that recruitment for the Division of Safeguards would be premature, since the Agency had not yet received any requests from governments or regional organizations to participate in control arrangements. "Therefore, any expenditure relating to the recruitment of staff for the Division would at present be useless."[38] It was the American view—supported by Canada and the United Kingdom—that it was "essential that the Agency should be prepared at an early date to discharge its statutory responsibilities."[39] Obviously, parties to bilateral agreements would not entrust the application of safeguards to the Agency until it was in a position to assume such a responsibility. The Agency would therefore have to begin its functions in that field as soon as possible. The debate, fundamentally fiscal in nature, continued through twenty-five meetings of the Board. Finally, on July 2, 1958, the Board, by a vote of 12-1, decided to staff the Division. The Soviet Union cast the only negative vote and nine Governors from the underdeveloped countries abstained.[40]

The growing friction between the superpowers in the IAEA came to a head in 1961. The specific issue was the election of a successor to Mr. Sterling Cole, Director-General of the IAEA, whose term expired in 1961. The United States proposed a Swedish national, Dr. Sigvard Eklund, as Director-General and defended the candidate largely on grounds of his excellent scientific qualifications. The Soviet Union, India, and the African states supported the candidacy of Dr. Sudjarwo, a national of Indonesia. In a bitter attack on the U.S. position, the Soviet Union advanced the view that since the first Director-General had been an American, the second should not be a national from a Western power; moreover, since the Agency operated largely for the benefit of the less developed nations, an Asian or African should be in a leading position; and finally, the Soviet delegate deplored the lack of consultation over the appointment of a successor to Mr. Cole. The IAEA General Conference was deeply split on the issue. Although Dr. Eklund's appointment was confirmed by a vote of 46-16, with 5 abstentions, the incoming Director-General faced a resentful minority led by the Soviet bloc and including India and several other members of the Afro-Asian group.

Superpower By-pass: The Agency in Limbo

While the three-cornered struggle between the United States, the USSR, and the underdeveloped countries has continued within the Agency, the national policies of the superpowers *outside* its framework have posed the greatest threat to its effective functioning. Both superpowers, with the United States in the lead, have shown a preference for bilateral and regional arrangements that have by-passed the Agency. A debasement of inspection standards initiated by the Soviet Union has aggravated the situation even further. A continuation of these superpower policies may yet turn the Agency into a cold-war casualty.

While the discussions creating the Agency had been in progress, the U.S. government had been negotiating a series of bilateral agreements with Western European, Asian, and Middle Eastern countries, promising them atomic power for peaceful purposes. These "bilaterals" were cheaper for the recipient, since the United States offered to pay inspection costs, whereas the IAEA charged a fee to defray the expenses of inspections. By the time the new Agency came into being, the United States had negotiated thirty-five bilateral agreements.

President Eisenhower's "Atoms-for-Peace" address in 1953 had implied that American bilateral programs were temporary arrangements and would be terminated when the Agency came into being. Yet the trend away from internationalism was not easy to reverse. Once again, a division had developed between the Executive and Legislative branches over the definition of the U.S. national interest. While the Executive Branch favored an international approach, the Congress was reluctant to transfer large amounts of fissionable material to an international organization which included the Soviet Union and its satellites. Congressional leaders preferred direct bilateral negotiations between the United States and the recipient countries, safeguarding American inspection rights. The State Department, during the period of "thaw" in the cold war that followed the death of Stalin, still continued to support the Agency. The nomination of Sterling Cole—a former U.S. congressman—for the post of Director-General may in part have been an attempt to make the Agency more attractive in the eyes of the Congress. However, continued pressure from the Congress, the intensification of the cold war, and the Soviet Union's considerable influence on the Agency's governing body changed the Executive's attitude toward IAEA. By the time the Agency had completed its first year of operations, the State Department had decided to give preferential treatment to bilateral and regional arrangements.

Thus, the U.S. government continued its bilateral program. By the end of 1958, forty-five such arrangements had been negotiated, and not one application had reached the IAEA. Director-General Cole, in a speech before the Atomic Industrial Forum in 1958, clearly identified U.S. policy as the cause of the Agency's decline:

> The bilateral agreements are the Achilles heel of the Agency. If the demands of nations for atomic assistance are to be met by bilateral assistance, IAEA cannot achieve its objectives. If IAEA is to continue, there must be a change in policy by the United States and other nuclear powers to give more preferential treatment to the Agency.[41]

Not only did the United States refuse to change its policy, but the Soviet Union entered the bilateral game in response to the American challenge and negotiated ten agreements of its own. To make its offers more appealing, the USSR inserted a "no-inspection" clause. It claimed that it would not interfere in the domestic jurisdiction of the recipient states. Thus, the competitive debasement of inspection standards had begun.

In 1959, the United States sold 30,000 kilograms of fissionable material to the six countries of the European Atomic Energy Community with neither IAEA nor American inspection requirements. The European countries insisted on and received the right of self-inspection, thus setting a precedent for similar self-inspection by an Eastern regional bloc. Then a second agreement was concluded with the seventeen countries of the Organization for European Economic Cooperation, with control standards again below those of the IAEA. In 1963, the United States decided to render assistance to India's nuclear reactor program, but reserved only a marginal future role for the IAEA.

By 1963, only a few applications had reached the UN agency. Meanwhile, a total of seventy-six nations were accommodated by bilateral and regional agreements with uneven inspection standards —some as rigorous as those set by the IAEA, some less rigorous, and some involving no control whatsoever. In June 1963, however, the Soviet Union reversed its earlier stand and accepted the principle of Agency safeguards. In 1964, the United States followed suit by offering to place most of its bilateral agreements under Agency controls and by inviting the IAEA to inspect a large nuclear reactor at Rowe, Massachusetts, hoping that the Soviet Union would follow suit in its own atomic policy. And the year 1965 saw the beginnings of a limited US-Soviet partnership in an even more highly charged arena: that of nuclear nonproliferation.

Superpower Partnership: The Nonproliferation Treaty

The struggle over the nuclear nonproliferation treaty went through two distinct phases. Between 1961 and 1965, the nonnuclear nations of the world steadily urged the superpowers to take the initiative in negotiating a nonproliferation treaty. The Soviet Union and the United States showed interest but found themselves unable to agree on an acceptable draft. In 1965, however, the pattern changed. An open partnership gradually developed between the two superpowers, which, for the next four years, attempted to "sell" a nonproliferation treaty to the nonnuclear nations. On June 12, 1968, they succeeded when the General Assembly "commended" a draft treaty on the nonproliferation of nuclear weapons by a vote of 95 in favor and 4 against, with 21 abstentions.[42] The two phases of this three-cornered struggle are well worth examining.

The origins of the treaty are found in an Irish draft resolution, submitted on November 17, 1961, which called upon all states, particularly those possessing nuclear weapons, to secure an international agreement under which nuclear states would agree not to relinquish control of nuclear weapons nor to transmit information necessary for their manufacture, and nonnuclear states would agree not to manufacture or otherwise acquire control of them. This proposal was adopted unanimously by the General Assembly on December 4, 1961.[43] Sweden suggested that, in addition, the Secretary-General inquire under what conditions nonnuclear states might be willing to bind themselves not to seek to acquire or themselves manufacture nuclear weapons in the future. The Soviet Union, having in mind West Germany, considered the Swedish proposal weak but nevertheless supported it. The United States opposed it on the grounds that it might jeopardize the right of collective self-defense. The major U.S. concern, of course, was NATO. The majority of the General Assembly approved of the Swedish proposal, hoping that it would facilitate agreement between the superpowers to suspend nuclear tests and to agree on other measures of arms control. The proposal was adopted by a vote of 58 to 10, with 23 abstentions.[44] That same year, the Assembly also endorsed the creation of a new negotiating forum for disarmament—the Eighteen-Nation Committee on Disarmament (ENDC)—comprising not only the then-nuclear powers and some of their respective allies in NATO and the Warsaw Pact, but also eight nonaligned nonnuclear powers that were to represent every region of the world. This Committee, meeting in Geneva, henceforth became the main forum for the deliberations over the nonproliferation treaty.[45]

Sixty-two governments responded to the Secretary-General's inquiry. Reciprocity was mentioned most frequently as the condition under which governments would adhere to the treaty. The Soviet Union showed particular concern about the adherence of West Germany.

Little progress was made in 1962, because the attention of the superpowers was absorbed by the Cuban missile crisis. In 1963, the Soviet Union attacked an American plan for the establishment of a NATO multilateral nuclear force (MLF) as contrary to the principle of nonproliferation. The United States saw no incompatibility between the proposed MLF and a nonproliferation treaty. These mutually exclusive positions remained the main obstacle to progress in 1964 and early 1965. Despite persistent prodding by the nonnuclear and nonaligned nations, both in the ENDC and in the United Nations, the Soviet Union and the United States refused to cooperate. The main difference between them remained the question of access to nuclear weapons through military alliances.

In mid-1965, the picture changed. First, the superpowers were beginning to enjoy the fruits of détente after they had agreed to a limited test-ban treaty in 1963. Second, in 1964, they had both been jolted by the first nuclear explosion on mainland China. Third, by 1965, it had become clear that at least twelve other nations were on the threshold of becoming nuclear powers: Japan, India, West Germany, Sweden, Italy, Canada, Israel, and, over a little longer period, Brazil, Switzerland, Spain, Yugoslavia, and the UAR. Fourth, the MLF project was abandoned by the United States, which removed the main source of Soviet opposition. Fifth, both superpowers wished to maintain open channels in spite of, or perhaps because of, the Vietnam war. And finally, both the United States and the Soviet Union were eager to show themselves receptive to the prodding of the nonnuclear and nonaligned countries. Thus, on June 15, 1965, the UN Disarmament Commission recommended by a vote of 83 to 1 that the ENDC "accord special priority" to a nonproliferation treaty. One month later, the ENDC reconvened in Geneva to hammer out the broad outlines of a treaty.

During the summer of 1965, the eight nonaligned members of the ENDC still held the initiative. They proposed five basic principles to guide the negotiations:

1. The treaty should be void of any loopholes for the direct or indirect proliferation of nuclear weapons in any form.
2. It should embody an acceptable balance of obligations of nuclear and nonnuclear powers.
3. It should be a step toward disarmament, particularly nuclear disarmament.
4. It should include acceptable and workable provisions to ensure its effectiveness.
5. It should not adversely affect the right of states to join in establishing nuclear free zones.

On November 23 these principles were adopted by the General Assembly, in a vote of 93 to 0, with 5 abstentions.[46] Both the United States and the Soviet Union voted for the resolution.

The year 1966 was a year of transition. Both superpowers began to work in earnest on a formula for a treaty. But they were deterred from assuming joint initiative by one stubborn problem, that of inspection. The Soviet Union favored the IAEA as the main inspection organ for the treaty, whereas the United States, under pressure from the Western European countries, preferred the European Atomic Energy Community (Euratom) as the inspection organ for its European allies. The Soviet Union accused the United States of trying to package two conflicting objectives: nonproliferation outside NATO and proliferation within NATO.

The United States was caught between its desire for a treaty and the demands of its allies in Western Europe for a nuclear voice. Gradually, the former assumed greater importance than the latter. The Soviet Union, for its part, felt a new urgency, since China had joined the nuclear club. Both superpowers, with an eye on the lengthening list of nuclear threshold powers, agreed that a nonproliferation treaty would have a stabilizing effect and that further delays might spur the nonnuclear countries to raise the price of their adherence.

In 1967 the superpowers assumed the initiative. In view of the stubborn disagreements surrounding the inspection provisions of the treaty, they agreed to disagree. On August 24, 1967, after intensive secret negotiations, they submitted separate but identical drafts in the ENDC, leaving blank the article that was to embody the inspection provision.

As the United States and the Soviet Union began to make a common front in late 1967, it was now the turn of the nonnuclear states to express reservations. As the discussions on the draft treaty began in the ENDC, all its members save Canada, Czechoslovakia, and Poland expressed reservations. The main issue that worried the nonnuclear powers was their security. India stated that she would sign only if she obtained guaranteed protection from both the United States and the Soviet Union. Most of the other members of the ENDC shared this view.

While presenting a common front vis-à-vis the nonnuclear states, the superpowers managed to settle on a compromise with regard to the thorny problem of safeguards. It was agreed that the IAEA verification procedures would ultimately apply to all nonnuclear states but that an inspection role would be maintained for Euratom during a transitional period.

On March 14, 1968, the ENDC submitted a full report of its deliberations to the General Assembly. This report contained the text of a complete draft treaty jointly submitted by the United

States and the Soviet Union as cochairmen of the ENDC. The draft included provisions for safeguards under Article 3.

The last stage of the struggle for General Assembly endorsement of the draft treaty was marked by a U.S.-Soviet partnership all the way. The two superpowers now lobbied hard for adoption of their joint product. Most of the reservations of the nonnuclear states continued to revolve around the problem of their own security. Many felt that the balance between the responsibilities of nuclear and nonnuclear states was not equitable because it was tilted against the latter. Many specific reservations were proposed by African, Asian, and Latin-American countries, all of which, in one form or another, expressed their displeasure with what they perceived as a double standard. These objections were met in part when the superpowers agreed to provide security assurances to the nonnuclear powers through a formal Security Council resolution.

Finally, on June 12, 1968, the General Assembly endorsed the treaty to halt the spread of nuclear weapons. The vote was 95 in favor, 4 against, 21 abstentions, and 4 not voting.[47] On June 19, 1968, the three nuclear powers on the Security Council gave their formal pledge to assist any nonnuclear country that was threatened by nuclear aggression. A resolution in the Council welcoming these pledges of assistance was passed by a vote of 10 in favor and 0 against, with 5 abstentions.[48] With this vote, the UN phase of the nonproliferation treaty came to an end.

The evolution of the U.S.-Soviet partnership during the late 1960's is reminiscent of the superpower negotiations over the IAEA statute more than a decade earlier. Once again, the Soviet Union's national interest as an atomic power dictated that the dispersion of atomic weapons be stopped. On the other hand, the USSR wished to appeal to the new nations, which perceived certain features of the treaty as an effort by the nuclear powers to impose a double standard. The United States, as the other leading atomic power, shared the USSR's interest in stopping proliferation. This common concern once again injected a high degree of harmony into U.S. relations with the Soviet Union. On the other hand, the United States had many difficulties with its Western European allies, some of which felt rather left out of the decision-making process. In fact, the United States faced at least as much friction over the treaty within the ranks of NATO as it did in its negotiations with its superpower adversary.

The nonnuclear nations, which in the early phases of the negotiations had spurred the superpowers to greater cooperation, wound up at the end with the uneasy feeling that something might have been put over on them. One happy though probably fortuitous by-product of this entire evolution was the gradual resuscitation of the International Atomic Energy Agency. First created by the superpowers, then by-passed and virtually ignored, the Agency was given a new lease on life when the superpowers managed to invest it with a significant role in the inspection procedures that were to govern the nonproliferation treaty. Thus, while the Agency was originally conceived in order to produce more atomic plowshares, its major purpose might yet become the blunting of the atomic sword.

Conclusions

Once again, as in the IRO case, the functionalist thesis does not stand up under scrutiny. On the issue of refugees, the superpowers negotiated, but one of them refused to join the new organization. On the issue of atoms for peace, the superpowers negotiated, joined the same Agency, but very shortly thereafter saw their national interests better served by going their own separate ways and by-passing the new Agency.

National-interest considerations also guided the superpowers both during the negotiating process and in their policies toward the Agency once it was established. During the first phase, the most striking aspect of superpower behavior was the unusual degree of harmony between them, owing to their partial common interest as atomic-producer powers vis-à-vis the have-nots of the world. Particularly interesting was the USSR's ambivalence in this role, since it also wanted to preserve its image of champion of the underdeveloped countries. Once the Agency came into being, however, both superpowers quickly turned away from it.

The IAEA was born in an American cradle, but the policy of by-passing it almost buried it in an American grave. The story is reminiscent of U.S. policy toward the League of Nations. At its heart were conflicting views between the Executive and Legislative branches as to what constituted the American national interest. The

Congress, which was largely instrumental in persuading the Executive into by-passing the Agency with bilateral agreements, saw the national interest primarily in terms of short-range gains against the Soviet Union in the cold war; it hoped to win the gratitude of the developing nations for atoms for peace given to them directly by the United States rather than through the medium of the world organization. The Executive, on the other hand, by at first favoring the IAEA, had more long-range goals in mind: to keep the USSR within the Agency framework and to set up a rigorous UN inspection system to be applied on a global basis. In short, the Executive saw the American national interest better served through the United Nations, whereas the Congress did not.

In the 1960's, during the American-Soviet détente, the pendulum began to swing back. The USSR started the process in 1963 and the United States followed suit the following year. By the late 1960's, both superpowers were sufficiently fearful of nuclear proliferation that they embarked on an open partnership in order to secure a treaty. In the process, the IAEA was granted important inspection responsibilities and thus received a new lease on life.

It is true that, unlike the IRO, the IAEA managed to attract almost universal membership. But while the IRO sacrificed universality to operational effectiveness, the IAEA's operational achievements so far have been modest. This comparison suggests a more general dilemma for a UN economic and social operation. A UN agency must serve some superpower national interest if it is to attract and hold superpower membership. But to attract both is to invite the East-West conflict into the day-to-day operations of the Agency which, in turn, may impede its effectiveness. Thus, by doing without one superpower's support, a UN agency may still be able to function effectively and perform useful services. The IRO is a case in point. However, if a UN agency tries to embrace both superpowers, it may find that the common denominator of cooperation is so low that more can be achieved outside the agency than inside it. Then, like the IAEA, the agency may be by-passed for long periods. Thus, universality of membership, while bringing certain benefits, must be balanced against the limits which the incorporation of different national interests will place on the agency's capacity to act.

SELECTED BIBLIOGRAPHY

Jessup, Philip C., and Howard J. Taubenfeld. *Controls for Outer Space*. New York: Columbia University Press, 1959.

Melman, Seymour, ed. *Inspection for Disarmament*. New York: Columbia University Press, 1958.

Noel-Baker, Philip. *The Arms Race*. New York: Oceana, 1958.

Spanier, John W., and Joseph L. Nogee. *The Politics of Disarmament: A study in Soviet-American Gamesmanship*. New York: Praeger, 1962.

Stoessinger, John G. "Atoms for Peace: The International Atomic Energy Agency," in Arthur N. Holcombe, ed., *Organizing Peace in the Nuclear Age*, pp. 117-233. New York: New York University Press, 1959.

Waltz, Kenneth N. *Man, the State, and War: A Theoretical Analysis*. New York: Columbia University Press, 1959.

CHAPTER 9

A United Nations Dilemma: Cuba and the Special Fund

The assistance furnished by the Special Fund . . . shall not be accompanied by any conditions of a political nature.
            Principles governing assistance
            furnished by the Special Fund.

The United States opposed this project when it was put up for approval in May 1961; we have reiterated our opposition on several occasions since; we are still opposed. Our policy toward Cuba involves opposition to any source of aid and comfort to the present regime. We pursue this policy in the United Nations and elsewhere by all means available to us.
            Statement by Richard N. Gardner
            U.S. Deputy Assistant Secretary
            of State for International
            Organization Affairs, Hearings on
            Special Fund, February 18, 1963.

Our concluding case study will concentrate on the behavior of one superpower, the United States, in the area of economic development. The UN's specialized agencies and voluntary programs have been active in this field. The specialized agencies most directly involved have been the World Health Organization, the Food and Agriculture Organization, the International Labour Organization, UNESCO, and, to a lesser extent, the IAEA discussed in the preceding chapter. The two voluntary programs have been the Expanded Program for Technical Assistance, launched in 1950, and the Special Fund, which began operations in 1959. In 1966 these two bodies were merged into the United Nations Development Program (UNDP). The specialized agencies have been financed through assessment; EPTA and the Special Fund have depended exclusively upon voluntary contributions from governments.

The two voluntary programs were largely the result of American initiative. The impetus for EPTA came out of Point Four of President Truman's inaugural speech of January 1949. Subsequently, the United States proposed to the UN Economic and Social Council that a concrete program be elaborated for enlarging technical assistance activities. Since 1950, when EPTA began operations with $20 million provided by 54 nations, contributions have steadily increased. In 1955, 70 nations pledged over $27 million. And by 1964, pledges from 108 governments exceeded $50 million. The United States contributed 60 percent of the total at first, but by 1964 it had reduced its share to 40 percent.

The Special Fund was set up in 1959 for the purpose of financing preparatory and "preinvestment" projects which would make it possible for technical assistance and development to yield optimum results. In keeping with its mandate, the Fund has concentrated on relatively large projects. The sum total of government contributions has exceeded that for EPTA—$38.5 million in 1960 and over $80 million in 1964. Again, the United States limits its contribution to 40 percent of the total. A dynamic force behind the drive for Special Fund resources has been Mr. Paul G. Hoffman, Managing Director of the Fund, and an American citizen.

The attitude of the Soviet Union toward the UN development programs has been ambivalent. During the lifetime of Stalin, the USSR largely ignored the UN voluntary programs or attacked them as imperialist dominated. Certainly, it did not contribute to them, since the aid went to countries which were generally "on the wrong side" of the revolution. With the ascendancy of Khrushchev, however, the Soviet attitude became more flexible. Opportunity beckoned in the developing countries of Asia, Africa, and the Middle East. Anticolonial passions could perhaps be exploited for the Soviet cause. Moreover, it had become clear that EPTA was not going to fail, that its popularity would increase, and more harm would come to the Soviet Union by remaining outside than by participating. Thus, as in their late participation in the IAEA, the

USSR in the mid-1950's rejoined most of the specialized agencies and began to make small contributions to EPTA amounting to somewhat less than 3 percent of the total. And when the Special Fund was established in 1959, the Soviet Union joined in its support with a similar contribution.

The evidence suggests that Soviet support of EPTA and the Special Fund was not motivated primarily by altruistic or humanitarian considerations. In the eyes of most recipient states, the two programs had become largely identified with the United States. This trend was clearly not in the Soviet national interest. The new Soviet leadership in the mid-1950's saw the voluntary programs as possible forums for Communist propaganda. The possible gains to be made by participating justified the making of small contributions via the United Nations to countries in the non-Communist world.

In their deliberations on development projects, EPTA's Technical Assistance Board and the Special Fund's Governing Council considered all their programs in private and submitted a package of projects to be approved in a single vote. This procedure was adopted from the very beginning in order to minimize political considerations in the decision-making process. On a number of occasions, the Soviet delegate to the Special Fund objected to projects in anti-Communist countries like Formosa, South Korea, and South Vietnam, but never forced a separate vote on any one given project. Similarly, the United States, *inter alia*, regularly approved projects in Communist countries like Poland and Yugoslavia.

Indeed, until 1960, neither EPTA nor the Special Fund was deeply affected by cold-war politics. It was the Cuban case that changed all this and set two interesting precedents. It marked the first time that the cold war intruded blatantly into UN economic-development programs. And, second, it placed the United States in a new and unfamiliar role. For the first time in the history of the United Nations, the United States found itself in the position of the single dissenter trying to cast a "veto," as it were, on an issue affecting its national interest. For the first time, the usual roles of the two superpowers were reversed: the Soviet Union, in the majority, was eagerly advocating a project, while the United States, in the minority, was resisting it.

Cuba and the Special Fund

The origin of the Special Fund project in Cuba came from Fidel Castro's request for aid at the time of his visit to the United Nations Fifteenth General Assembly in September 1960. The Cuban government saw the need for the diversification of agriculture in order to reduce its dependence upon its sugar crop. Accordingly, with the help of an FAO expert acting as the representative of the Managing Director of the Special Fund, it formulated a project proposal. Managing Director Paul Hoffman, acting upon the proposal, recommended to the Special Fund's Governing Council that twelve UN experts and some equipment be sent to the agricultural station at Santiago de las Vegas to study the fields of tropical animal husbandry, soil classification, conservation, and crop diversification.

The proposed project was to last five years. It called for an allocation from the Special Fund of $1,157,000, including a cash contribution from Cuba of $114,500. The Cuban government was to make available a counterpart contribution of personnel, services, land, and buildings in the equivalent of $1,878,000. The total Cuban contribution was thus to be $1,992,500, and the total cost to the Special Fund $1,042,500. The Food and Agriculture Organization was designated as the executing agency of the project.

The project came up for formal approval before the Governing Council of the Special Fund in May 1961, a few weeks after the disastrous Bay of Pigs invasion. Needless to say, the American attitude toward Cuba was not conducive to approval of a project to aid Castro's island. Yet, when the Special Fund was created, it had been agreed that political considerations would play no part in the allocation of aid; projects were to be determined according to economic criteria. This stipulation had been carefully honored. The United States had agreed to projects in Communist countries; the Soviet Union had accepted aid projects to Taiwan and South Korea; and Egypt had acquiesced in one to Israel.

Nevertheless, American policy toward Cuba now was to oppose "any source of aid and comfort to the present regime."[1] The United States thus decided to oppose the project, but on economic rather than political grounds. When the project was brought before the Governing Council in May, U.S. representative Philip Klutznick stated the American objections. He noted that projects should be chosen according to certain criteria established by the Managing Director, among them: (1) the urgency of the recipient country's need; (2) the prospect that the project would lead to early results, have a wide impact on the country, and lead to new capital investment; (3) the certainty that the project would enjoy the full cooperation of the recipient government, with trained personnel; and (4) the government's assumption of responsibility upon completion of the project. Mr. Klutznick then pointed out that "recent developments in Cuba [had] raised substantial question as to whether the above-mentioned criteria [could be] satisfied with respect to the project before us." He specified four developments which, in his view, would frustrate the objectives of the Cuban project, and therefore led him to suggest its rejection. These developments were: (1) Cuba had failed to take advantage of existing multilateral sources of technical assistance through the OAS; (2) the Cuban government had displaced or driven into exile qualified personnel at the same time that it had requested UN technicians to replace them; (3) the wholesale slaughter of livestock and misuse of other physical resources had raised doubts about the utility of any aid in livestock-raising techniques; (4) the existence of a bilateral technical assistance agreement with the Soviet bloc which would bring 300 agricultural experts to Cuba had mitigated the urgency of the need for the UN project. Adding that political and economic conditions were interrelated and that the manner in which a country was governed had economic consequences, Mr. Klutznick concluded that the U.S. opposition was not based on political considerations:

> Mr. Chairman, for the reasons I have stated, this project has not received the approval of my government. We have great respect for the judgment of the staff of the Special Fund. Under normal procedures, the Managing Director would examine any questions arising before entering into a plan of operations for any project. We are confident, therefore, that the project will not proceed until the staff has satisfied itself

about the questions we have raised and is certain that the
project can be completed successfully to the ultimate benefit
of the Cuban people.[2]

Hence, the basic American argument in 1961 was that the Cuban
government had so subordinated the economic and social welfare
of the Cuban people to the narrow political aims of its leadership
that the minimum standards of efficiency and effectiveness which
must guide the implementation of cooperative development projects—whether in the UN system or without—could not possibly be
met.[3]

The United States felt that its national interest could not permit the Cuban project, and undertook a major diplomatic effort
to block its recommendation in the Governing Council. Working
against the United States was the general practice of the Council
never to have a separate vote on any one project, but rather to
vote on the whole package of proposals by the Managing Director.
Moreover, many delegates on the Council felt that the economic
arguments advanced by the United States against the Cuban project
were thinly disguised political ones. Thus, when the United States
tried to round up seven votes, the necessary blocking third in the
eighteen-member Council, it discovered that the other members
were unwilling to aid in the precedent-breaking consideration of
a single project. They were afraid lest this might lead the Soviet
Union to force separate votes on aid to Taiwan, South Korea, and
South Vietnam, or Egypt on aid to Israel. There was general concern that approval of individual projects would turn the Special
Fund into an East-West battleground.

In later testimony before the Senate Subcommittee of the Committee on Foreign Relations in 1963, State Department officials
explained U.S. policy. Since the United States could not obtain the
necessary seven votes to block the Cuban project, it decided not
to press for a losing vote. Instead, it settled for going on record
against the project, hoping that Paul Hoffman might be dissuaded
from the project by other means. Hence, in May 1961, the Cuban
project was approved, along with all the others.

The Managing Director now found himself in a dilemma. He
was an international civil servant, but also a prominent American
citizen. It was his duty to proceed with the project, once approved

by the Governing Council, unless there were economic considerations to the contrary. He was under continual pressure from both Washington and Havana. The project hung fire for over a year and a half, while Hoffman investigated whether there were any valid economic reasons for canceling it. He could find none. Also, as one observer put it:

> Hoffman thought the political objections more emotional than rational. The proposed project was so minute and so long range that it could not possibly have any significant effect on Castro's tenure in office.

> If the United States could not get rid of the dictator in the six to eight years before the project would come to fruition, diplomats pointed out to him, Washington probably would never be able to. Twelve men studying Cuban soil use could not remotely affect the outcome.[4]

On February 13, 1963, the United Nations announced that it would proceed with the agricultural project in Cuba. Hoffman made one concession, however: the five-year program would be reviewed after six months and only five men would be sent to Cuba to study how the country might diversify its agriculture. If conditions proved propitious for the project and if the Cuban government did not renege on its responsibilities and sharing of the costs, then the other seven experts would be sent and the project would be put into full operation.

The reaction in the United States to Mr. Hoffman's decision was one of anger. The press was almost unanimous in its disapproval and a Senate Subcommittee of the Committee on Foreign Relations began an investigation of the Special Fund project. The Senators wanted to know why the United States had not pressed for a reconsideration of the Cuban project at the January 1963 meeting of the Governing Council.

Mr. Richard N. Gardner, Deputy Assistant Secretary of State for International Organization Affairs, explained that reconsideration to suspend the project required a two-thirds vote. Despite the shift of Latin-American opinion after the Punta del Este Conference of January 1962, and the more recent opposition to Cuba arising out of the missile crisis of the fall of 1962, a canvass had indicated that the necessary number of votes could not be obtained. Thus the United States had again decided not to bring the issue to a vote. Instead, it was the American hope that, owing to the economic and technical objections raised by Mr. Klutznick, the project would not be implemented. Moreover, it was feared that a public statement might create an uproar that would force Mr. Hoffman to authorize the full operation immediately.

Most of the senators, however, were of the opinion that the United States should have pressed for a vote, despite the possibility of losing. In addition, they suggested another reason for opposing the project—Cuba's delinquency in its payments to the United Nations. Although Cuba had pledged $55,000 to the Special Fund for the 1960-1963 period, it had made no actual payment. It had paid none of its UNEF and ONUC assessments, nor its pledges to EPTA assistance—over $800,000 for the period 1961-1964. Finally, it was pointed out that Cuba was a year in arrears on its regular budget assessment.

Mr. Gardner replied that these points had been raised in January 1963, but that they had not impressed the necessary two-thirds of the Council's membership. He then forcefully stated the reason for not pressing for a vote that the United States was sure to lose:

> If we had forced it to a vote it would have been the first time in history, in the history of the Special Fund, that a division was had on an individual project, and it would have meant that hereafter the Soviets would have forced a vote on all the projects in Taiwan, South Korea, in Vietnam, which they do not like, and we would have been, if I may put it this way, jeopardizing the 97 per cent of the Special Fund projects we do like for the sake of 3 per cent which we do not like.[5]

The Senate Subcommittee hearings also brought out some interesting statistics about the Special Fund aid in general. The Communist bloc, including Yugoslavia, had paid $8 million into the Fund, but had received in projects to Communist countries only $6 million. That is to say, the Communist bloc had paid 3 percent of the Fund's capital but received only 2½ percent of the Fund's allocations. And the Communist bloc had been the recipient of six out of a total of 288 projects, that is, slightly more than 2 percent. Mr. Gardner's fear of jeopardizing the 97 percent of Special Fund projects that were backed by the United States was thus very understandable, even though his argument omitted the fact that the United States probably had the voting power on the Governing Council to push through most of the projects it desired by separate votes if it had to. Moreover, all but five countries aided by the Special Fund were also recipients of direct aid from the United States. Hence, a reduction of Special Fund aid to these countries as a result of Soviet pressure might merely have increased the necessity of more direct American aid. Indeed, Cuba was the only Communist country receiving Special Fund aid which the United States did not help in some way. Poland and Yugoslavia received both Special Fund and direct American assistance.

Thus, the first time a Special Fund project went directly against the American interest, the U.S. Congress decided to make an issue of it, although the project represented only one-half of 1 percent of total Special Fund aid. If the Executive had followed suit and the American delegation on the Governing Council had pressed for a vote, the tradition of consensus governing that body's decision-making process would have been broken. The USSR would then probably have called for separate votes on other projects. While the United States probably could have won most of these votes, the cold war would nevertheless have been introduced into UN economic development.

The actual decision to acquiesce alienated Congressional opinion and called into question the continuance of the large American contribution to the Fund and other UN aid operations by focusing on the single project which was not in the U.S. interest. The vehemence of the opposition brought the cold war into the Special Fund anyway, even though no separate vote was actually forced. The Subcommittee hearings made it plain that a separate vote was not taken only because the United States would have lost. The United States had not merely registered its disapproval of an unpopular project, as the Soviet Union had done, but had pressed for its removal both behind the scenes and in public.

On balance, the Congress defended the short-range national interest of the United States: its position was largely influenced by pressure from constituencies for satisfaction against Cuba. The Executive was less impressed with the short-run gains against Cuba and more with the long-range losses to American interest if the United States had disrupted the nonpolitical voting tradition of the Special Fund.

Perhaps the most important element affecting this American dilemma was the tenor of the times. The timing of the project was unfortunate. As one correspondent put it: "A very large segment of American opinion screamed whenever the word Cuba was mentioned. Especially after the missile crisis, the very idea of aiding Castro with so much as a garden trowel was anathema to them and to Congress."[6]

An interesting postscript to the Cuban project is that six months after its inception, the Special Fund quietly put it on a regular five-year basis. This fact caused hardly a ripple in American Congressional and public opinion.

Conclusions

The Cuban case shows that, in the United States, the Executive and Congress may be deeply split in their perceptions of the American national interest in the United Nations. In both the Secretariat case discussed in Chapter 3 and the problem of UN finances examined in Chapter 6, Congressional pressure tends toward a more short-range view of the national interest that is often in conflict with long-range American objectives in the United Nations. In the Cuban case, the split was profound. The view of the Administration was best expressed in the following statement by Mr. Gardner:

> The price of participating in any political institution is that you cannot get your way all the time. We cannot expect to get our way all the time in the United Nations. There will be entries on the debit as well as on the credit side of the ledger. The central question is whether the credits exceed the debits—whether looking at the balance sheet as a whole the institution is making a net contribution to our national interest. The United States Government continues to believe that the answer to that question is overwhelmingly in the affirmative.[7]

As a result, the State Department preferred not to force the Cuban project to a vote. Many members of the Congress, however, under heavy pressure from their constituencies, found it difficult to justify "American money going via the United Nations to Cuba," and impossible to explain the complexities of the situation to the electorate.

When considered in the broader context of superpower interaction in the United Nations, the Cuban case puts in serious question the validity of the functionalist thesis: that the sphere of economic cooperation may be insulated from the storms of political controversy and that it may even be used as a stepping stone toward the building of political order. Indeed, the relationship of the two superpowers in the Special Fund suggests an inversion of the functionalist proposition. Certainly, Soviet participation in that body was not inspired by a desire for greater East-West accord, but by the fear of Western gains in the uncommitted countries and the reluctance to concede leadership in technical-assistance activities to the United States.

The United States, in turn, has supported Special Fund programs, but only so long as most of these have been in accord with America's own national interest. The Cuban project demonstrated that, for the United States, too, it has proved impossible to separate economic from political considerations. When a development project was seen by the Congress as inimical to the American interest, the Government was almost pressured into taking an even tougher line than the Soviet Union did in comparable situations.

Most important, perhaps, the Cuban case placed the United States in a minority position for the first time on an issue which the nation saw as clearly inimical to its national interest. And it showed that the United States, when placed in such a situation, faces severe Congressional pressures that may yet compel it to fight the majority as fiercely and stubbornly as the Soviet Union. It suggests the possibility that the depth of the American commitment to the United Nations is yet to be tested. The Soviet Union has been a permanent minority since the beginning of the United Nations; the United States, on the other hand, has had very little experience with hostile majorities in the United Nations. In that sense, the Cuban case may be a harbinger of things to come in a changing United Nations.

SELECTED BIBLIOGRAPHY

Asher, Robert E., and Associates. *The United Nations and the Promotion of the General Welfare.* Washington, D.C.: The Brookings Institution, 1957.

Gardner, Richard N., and Max F. Millikan, eds. *The Global Partnership.* New York: Praeger, 1968.

Jacobson, Harold K. *The USSR and the UN's Economic and Social Activities.* Notre Dame, Ind.: University of Notre Dame Press, 1963.

Laves, Walter H. C., and Charles A. Thompson. *UNESCO: Purpose, Progress, Prospects.* Bloomington: Indiana University Press, 1957.

Mitrany, David. *A Working Peace System.* Chicago: The Quadrangle Press, 1966.

Myrdal, Gunnar. *An International Economy.* New York: Harper & Row, 1956.

Sewell, James Patrick. *Functionalism and World Politics.* Princeton, N.J.: Princeton University Press, 1966.

Sharp, Walter R. *Field Administration in the United Nations System.* New York: Praeger, 1961.

———. *International Technical Assistance.* Chicago: Public Administration Service, 1952.

———. *The Economic and Social Council.* New York: Columbia University Press, 1969.

PART IV

Conclusions

CHAPTER 10

——◆◆◆——

The United Nations
and the Superpowers

*The crisis of our loyalty to the United Nations is still ahead
of us.*

Adlai E. Stevenson
*U.S. Representative to
the United Nations, 1962.*

The conflict between the two superpowers has dominated international politics since World War II and, naturally, has cast its shadow over the United Nations. The split between the United States and the Soviet Union quickly destroyed many of the basic assumptions on which the United Nations had been founded. For example, the assumption that the UN's peace-keeping strength could be based on the unity of the great powers collapsed almost immediately. Since that time the United Nations has passed through a succession of dark nights of the soul: the Soviet walkouts, the Korean "police" action, the American attack on the Secretariat, the simultaneous crises in Hungary and Suez, the ten-year membership stalemate, the Congo crisis, the Soviet *troika* attack, coupled with the tragic death of Secretary-General Hammarskjöld and the dispute over payments for peace-keeping operations. At each crisis there have been prophets of doom claiming that the United Nations was living on borrowed time and predicting that *this* time the Organization, like the League before it, would finally go under. Yet the United Nations has weathered each crisis and, far from going under, has appeared to grow stronger with the years.

If the United Nations has not been living on borrowed time, even its advocates must admit that it has been living on borrowed money. The issues at stake in the peace-keeping crisis have not been resolved with finality despite the American decision to drop the fight over the application of Article 19. For this reason, the outcome of the 1964-1965 crisis over the payment of assessments for peacekeeping operations was one of the most important watersheds in the Organization's history. It determined how much of its past was to be consolidated for use in the future. Some leading contemporary analysts were far from hopeful. In March 1965 Professor Hans Morgenthau found that "the Security Council [was] powerless, the General Assembly [was] powerless, and the Secretary-General [was] powerless. The United Nations has ceased to be an effective international organization."[1] In short, while Professor Morgenthau might admit that before the financing crisis the United Nations had appeared to grow stronger over the years, in 1965 he suggested that this growth had not only been halted but cut back severely.

From the perspective of the preceding nine chapters, it seems that in order to survive for the past twenty-five years, the United Nations has had to learn one vital lesson: how to deal with the superpowers. The interaction between the United States and the Soviet Union has been central to the UN's development. This book has examined this interaction in the constitutional, peace-keeping, and economic and social fields of UN activity. In each of these areas the relationship between the United Nations and the superpowers has revealed certain basic themes. First, the superpowers' national interest has been the major determinant of their policies toward the United Nations; when the United Nations serves that interest, the Organization is allowed to go forward; when it does not, its evolution is hindered. Second, the United Nations has dealt with these clashing national interests in a pragmatic and flexible manner. Third, through this flexible policy, the United Nations has emerged from a harrowing series of crises as a stronger force in international politics. The extent of that progress in each of the fields noted above will now be evaluated.

Constitutional Evolution

The major theme that emerges from the analysis in Part I is the controlling role that the superpowers' national interest has played in the evolution of the United Nations. We have noted the decisive impact of superpower policies on three major UN organs: the Security Council, the General Assembly, and the Secretariat. In analyzing the use of the veto in the Security Council, we have seen that among the most effective Soviet vetoes have been the ones employed in direct defense of the USSR's national interest in confrontations with the West. The United States, for its part, has developed an equally effective though less conspicuous "hidden veto" with which to guard its vital interests. The struggle over membership policy in the General Assembly showed the United States first defending a policy of exclusion, which resulted in its retention of an automatic majority. The USSR pressed for "package deals" that would have improved its relative voting position. After 1955, both superpowers saw their interests better served by opening wide the gates of admission in order to cultivate the newly emergent nations. The case study on the Secretariat demonstrated that each superpower was prepared to attack that Office when it saw danger to its national interest, although the American attack was led by the Congress, not the Executive.

On the whole, the three case studies support the contention that the United States has been more successful in the pursuit of its national interest in the United Nations than the Soviet Union. Our examination of the USSR's "absolute" weapon, its 105 vetoes, revealed that only 24 of these had conclusively prevented further action. Twenty-five had been "circumvented" by compensatory UN action, often under American pressure, and 56, including the 43 membership vetoes, had been superseded through direct negotiations.

On the other hand, the American "hidden veto" has thus far remained an effective weapon, although its edge was somewhat blunted by the enlargement of the Security Council in 1966. And, although the USSR attempted to use a variant of the Uniting for Peace procedure in the wake of the Arab-Israeli war of 1967, it was unable to muster a two-thirds majority for its position. Our case study on membership showed that, although the United States did suffer a setback when it lost its automatic two-thirds majority after the "package deal" of 1955, it has managed to avoid defeat on vital issues. The issue of Chinese representation is a case in point. Finally, the attack on the Secretariat emanating from the

United States was in the main successful, whereas the Soviet assault was a failure.

There are three basic reasons that explain the greater degree of American success. First, the United States still has a larger number of allies in all UN organs, while the USSR is still in a minority. Second, the large American financial contribution to the budgets of the UN system has given that nation an important measure of bargaining power in negotiations regarding the Organization's activities. Finally, the United States, unlike the Soviet Union, has a tradition in politics of lobbying and the building of parliamentary majorities. And since most UN business is transacted in a parliamentary framework, the United States may have enjoyed a tactical advantage.

The second major theme evident in Part I is the extraordinary flexibility demonstrated by the UN's principal organs. In response to various challenges, the United Nations has shifted power pragmatically to the organ most free to cope with the particular crisis. In this manner, the locus of power has moved from the Security Council to the General Assembly and the Secretary-General and back again to the Security Council. The Organization has responded to political problems in a political manner, relying heavily on the arts of improvisation and compromise. In this sense, the United Nations contrasts sharply with the League of Nations, which was unable to muster any countervailing forces when confronted by threats from the future Axis powers and the Soviet Union. Three of the major UN organs have exercised important international responsibilities, and in a crisis some precedent would exist for their use. Or else, the United Nations, by applying its "flexible-response" doctrine, might devise an entirely new solution. In short, like any living institution, the United Nations has remained resilient.

Upon reflection, one can see that these two themes—national interest and the UN's evolution through flexibility—are interconnected. The UN's evolution has been forced in part by the pressure of the superpowers' striving to achieve their national interests. For example, the U.S.-Soviet struggle was primarily responsible for shifting the locus of power within the UN system. In 1950, the United States, eager to circumvent the Soviet veto, persuaded the General Assembly to pass the Uniting for Peace Resolution, which broadened that organ's mandate in peace and security matters. The United States saw its interest better served in an Assembly that its allies controlled than in a veto-bound Security Council. In 1956, again as a result of American initiative and, significantly, after the first increase in membership, the locus of power moved from the Assembly to the Office of the Secretary-General. The large influx of new members in the Assembly that had been actively sought by the Soviet Union had cost the United States its automatic majority. Hence, the United States encouraged the passage of broadly conceived resolutions that invested the Secretary-General with increasing policy-making responsibilities. The subsequent Soviet attack on the Office in 1960 was an attempt to eliminate that increased responsibility. Beginning in 1961, after the "troika's" failure was evident, the Soviet Union exercised more restraint in its use of the veto. By so doing, the USSR could retain some authority over an operation in the Council rather than lose it to the Assembly or to the Secretary-General. Thus, the Security Council was resuscitated as a major UN power center.

Hence, the first three case studies suggest that the superpowers' quest for national interest through the United Nations and the development of the international organization itself may not necessarily be contradictory. On the most practical level, if the United Nations did not serve *some* national interest of the superpowers, it would be ignored by them. To be relevant in world politics, the United Nations must be used; to be used, it must serve. Part of the price of relevance, therefore, is service. On a deeper level, however, we have also seen that if the superpowers are going to use the United Nations to promote their national interests, they must first give it sufficient power and authority to act. Once given, this power cannot always be so easily withdrawn. For example, in order to use the General Assembly in peace and security operations, the United States broadened its mandate through the Uniting for Peace Resolution. Today this procedure is theoretically available to any group that can muster the requisite majority. The participation of the Secretary-General in the Suez crisis, a role that the Soviet Union did not actively oppose, made it natural in the Congo crisis to turn once again to the Secretary-General, whom the USSR later opposed violently. In short, some residue of authority seems to remain with the United Nations even after the super-powers' immediate goals are met. Hence, one can picture the United Nations as a midget caught between two giants—being used and abused by each in turn—but all the while stealing strength from each. And since the superpowers frequently attempt to use the United Nations against each other, it appears that part of the UN's growth in strength has actually taken place *because* of super-power conflict as well as in spite of it.

Peace-Keeping Operations

In Part II we examined the superpowers' role in the establishment, political control, and financial support of two major UN peace-keeping operations. One striking similarity between UNEF and ONUC was the environment in which each crisis developed. In each case a local dispute escalated into a conflict between na-tionalism and colonialism that, in turn, led to a major confrontation between the superpowers. With each phase, the conflict became wider and more dangerous. The speed of the escalation process was in part a result of a pattern of mutual exploitation among the various actors involved. The new nations sought support by raising the specter of colonialism, which brought in the Soviet Union in an attempt to exploit the situation by using these appeals for help as a pretext for intervention. Since the United States could not stand idly by, superpower involvement became inevitable. But at the outset of both crises, the United States and the USSR both saw their interests better served through UN action than through direct conflict.

The superpowers' national interests played a vital role in both peace-keeping operations. In the case of UNEF, the United States sought to extricate its allies, Britain and France, from their em-barrassing positions and to remove any pretext for Soviet inter-vention in the Middle East. Unilateral American action would have aroused the misgivings of the Afro-Asian nations and provided an excuse for a similar Soviet move. Hence, the United States fa-vored a UN buffer force as an instrument of neutralization. The Soviet national interest was not as clear-cut. On the one hand, the embarrassment to the U.S.'s two traditional allies and the subsequent reverberations in NATO were a singular coup. So was the expulsion of much of Anglo-French influence from the Middle East. Moreover, the action helped to bolster the Soviet image as champion of the underdeveloped world. On the other hand, however, the United Nations effectively negated any Soviet excuse for intervention and, besides, the General Assembly was conducting the operation under the auspices of the Uniting for Peace procedure, in violation of the Soviet view of the Charter. Thus, the USSR abstained from the initial vote authorizing UNEF, looking the other way while the Uniting for Peace procedure was invoked against the two Western powers, and it limited its objections to nonpayment of assessments. Although the two superpowers had very different motives, they both permitted the establishment of UNEF which, in turn, helped maintain a truce on the Israeli-Egyptian border for over a decade.

The superpowers' national interests also led them to favor the creation of ONUC, thus launching that operation in an atmosphere of consensus. The USSR voted for the establishment of ONUC, since it was eager to speed the withdrawal of the "colonialist" Belgian forces and to enable the Lumumba government to establish control. Once again, the United States wanted to interpose the United Nations between East and West and to prevent the Congo from becoming another cold-war battleground. Both superpowers recognized that the African states massively favored United Nations, rather than superpower, intervention, which was another reason for standing clear. Thus, the United States and the USSR, though their basic objectives in the Congo clashed, permitted the Security Council to act.

When the Congolese government broke down and the Soviet favorite was overcome by a more pro-Western candidate, the superpower consensus dissolved. The Security Council was stymied by the veto and the General Assembly carried on ONUC against the active opposition of the Soviet Union. But when seceded Katanga continued its rebellion, a partial consensus was restored in the Council. The superpowers, again for very different reasons, approved two of the strongest resolutions in the Council's history in order to end the secession.

The financial crisis over UNEF and ONUC was a reflection of

the political crisis, and hence also deeply influenced by the superpowers' national interests. In the case of UNEF, the Soviet interest
dictated only mild criticism of the operation and therefore nonpayment of assessments. But in the later stages of ONUC, the
USSR felt its national interest directly jeopardized; hence, an attack on the Secretary-General and an attempt to act unilaterally
in the Congo, as well as complete refusal to pay for ONUC, followed. From the Soviet point of view, UNEF and ONUC prevented
Soviet bridgeheads in the Middle East and Africa. In the latter case,
since a bridgehead had already been established and was liquidated
at least in part under UN pressure, Soviet opposition assumed a
more violent form. In neither case was the USSR willing to pay
for an operation that did not favor its national interest.

It may be legitimate at this point to raise a hypothetical question: Would the United States pay for an operation that did not
favor its national interest? If Lumumba instead of Kasavubu had
been victorious in the Congo, would the United States have continued to support ONUC? Or suppose the Afro-Asian majority
backed by the Soviet Union recommended the creation of a UN
peace force to "establish order" in Angola and to expel the Por-
tuguese? Had such an operation been initiated by circumventing
an American veto in the Security Council and overcoming vigorous
American opposition in the General Assembly, one wonders if the
United States would still pay one-third of the expenses. In short,
if the national interest so dictates, the United States might some
day find itself opposing a UN peace-keeping action, while the
USSR urged the UN forward.

Perhaps the toughest problem for the United Nations in the realm
of peace and security is how to deal with the opposition of the
superpowers. It seems, in this connection, that the distinction between active and passive opposition may be crucial. If opposition
remains limited to nonpayment, as was the Soviet opposition to
UNEF, the other superpower may risk overriding it, provided the
money can be found to pay the share of the recalcitrant power.
But if more active obstruction is overridden, then the obstructionist
power may consider the United Nations too inimical to its national
interest and abandon it altogether. In short, it seems that the
launching of an operation in the face of either active or passive

opposition is to ask for a financial crisis. No great power, least of all a superpower, will adopt, or easily acquiesce in paying for, a policy that it considers inimical to its national interest, and those overriding the opposition may have to face the responsibility of assuming additional financial burdens.

An interesting point emerges from a comparison of UNEF with ONUC; although the superpowers' interests in both the Congo and the Middle East were not compatible, the United Nations managed to launch peace-keeping forces. At the outset of an operation, therefore, it would seem that basically antithetical interests need not necessarily preclude concrete UN action. However, as an operation evolves, it may become difficult to maintain the consensus and to collect payment.

The delicate task of acquiring and sustaining superpower support for peace-keeping operations falls to the United Nations itself and, particularly, to the Secretary-General. The key to the UN's success in the peace-keeping field—as in the realm of constitutional development discussed in Part I—has been flexibility. UNEF, as we have seen, needed the support and tacit consent respectively of the United States and the USSR in order to be launched. But since one purpose of the operation was to insulate the Middle East from a superpower conflict, it was necessary to exclude both superpowers from direct participation in the operation. Hence, UNEF meant a curious inversion of the UN Charter. The original belief of the founding fathers at San Francisco had been that concerted action by the great powers in any potential conflict would be necessary to preserve the peace. Now it seemed that concerted action would have to be taken to exclude the great powers from any potential conflict if the peace was to be preserved. Though the superpowers would have to give their blessings to the operation, they would at the same time have to be kept at arm's length.

In ONUC, too, superpower consensus launched the operation, but exclusion of the superpowers became necessary in order to sustain the peace-keeping force. One of the most difficult periods in that complex operation came when the Soviet Union began to introduce personnel and materiel into the Congo. The UN's flexibility in establishing ONUC without the physical participation of the superpowers seemed even more impressive when one observed the sensitive diplomatic maneuvers employed by the Secretary-General in readjusting ONUC's basis of support as the attitudes of the superpowers and of other nations changed during the course of the operation. From start to finish, ONUC was an outstanding example of UN flexible diplomacy.

Yet, upon reflection, can one account for the success of UNEF and, especially, ONUC solely on the grounds of the UN's flexibility? The United Nations did receive a certain amount of "delegated" strength from the superpowers to deal with the crisis, and the Organization used that strength flexibly and intelligently. But certain facts suggest that, once this mandate was granted, the UN operation developed additional strength of its own. This fact emerges with greatest clarity in the case of ONUC, where the attempts to limit the UN's actions were formidable. Of the five permanent members of the Security Council, the Soviet Union was violently opposed for considerable periods and refused to pay anything at all while the operation was in progress; China was indifferent, and unable to support the operation financially owing to lack of resources; Britain disapproved of parts of the operation sufficiently to withhold weapons from ONUC forces; France's political opposition was strong and it refused to pay its assessment; and in the United States, influential elements in the Congress and the Executive were increasingly ambivalent about UN policy toward Katanga and concerned with the high cost of the entire operation. Thus, at various times ONUC had almost all the Big Five, in addition to other, smaller, powers ranged against it. Where did the strength to continue come from?

Once again, it is important to distinguish between the kinds of opposition a UN operation may face. Passive or semiactive opposition by minor or even major powers can be endured. But in case of violent superpower opposition a UN operation needs an equally strong countervailing force in order to survive. Now when, with the rise of Kasavubu, the Soviet Union violently opposed ONUC, the United States had an equally strong interest in seeing it continued. Hence, a countervailing force was generated which helped sustain the operation. More broadly, in assessing the politics of survival for a given UN peace-keeping action, it is important to consider not only who is opposed, but how strongly opposed and what countervailing forces are created. As a political rule of thumb the United Nations might ask the questions: Who is mad? and how mad? Who is glad? and how glad?

On balance, it would seem therefore that once a UN peace-keeping operation is launched by superpower consensus, it can acquire a certain amount of independent strength and momentum. In the cases of UNEF and ONUC, at least part of this momentum was supplied by the strong backing of the newly emergent nations in the General Assembly. The United Nations has not only stolen strength from the two giants, but on occasion has gained enough additional strength to maneuver somewhat independently.

The Secretary-General has played a crucial role in this development. Political sense, timing, and flexibility have been his major weapons. A UN peace-keeping action may have enemies, but not too many enemies at the same time. The superpowers must approve initially, but must not participate physically. As the operation develops, its original consensus may change, and the Secretary-General must weigh carefully the often conflicting demands of the superpowers, the participating states, other UN members, and his obligations as an international civil servant and defender of the UN Charter. Moreover, the Secretary-General must find some way to pay for the operations.

In the financial crisis over the UNEF and ONUC assessments, the moderate amounts of money at issue were soon obscured by the larger political and constitutional implications. Many states, including the two superpowers, revealed their basic positions on the United Nations in the course of the negotiations. In fact, the 1964-1965 financing crisis clearly illustrated the three major themes we have noted in the course of this book: the dominance of national interest; the flexibility of the UN system; and the slow accretion of UN strength.

First, while the financial crisis was plainly the result of the clashing superpower national interests over UNEF and ONUC, the stalemate in the Nineteenth Assembly nevertheless revealed that both superpowers did find value in the UN system as a whole. For example, the Soviet Union hinted that it might make some payment on its debt in an effort to reach a compromise that would allow the United Nations to function normally again. And the United States, which insisted that the Soviets could not vote until they paid, did relent and permitted "consultations" and one procedural vote. Even the Afro-Asians permitted a year of deadlock and inaction in economic and social affairs rather than precipitate a showdown. In sum, almost everyone, including the superpowers, made compromises in an effort to keep the United Nations in being. This was best seen in the united front which all states, led by the United States and the USSR, took against the Albanian attempt to force a showdown. Thus, while the superpowers did not agree on the UN's exact nature, they indicated by their behavior that they did want *some* kind of United Nations.

Second, the flexibility of the UN system was certainly demonstrated during the Nineteenth Assembly. One ingenious scheme after another was concocted in order to avoid a showdown. All sides worked at length to find a compromise formula, and when that failed, a "no voting" scheme and various other expedients were devised to allow the Assembly to conduct part of its business without bringing the issue to a vote.

Third, the effects on the United Nations of the American decision to drop the fight over Article 19 have been complex. First, the outcome of the crisis has no doubt affected the gains of the United Nations in one major area—that of peace-keeping. While this is a key area, one should not forget that the Organization makes contributions in dozens of other important ways. Second, those peace-keeping operations that directly involve the East-West struggle have been the ones most directly affected. And third, it seems clear that the principle of collective financial responsibility for peace-keeping operations voted by the General Assembly over the active opposition of a superpower has fallen into disfavor. Agreement of the superpowers has been sought instead; and, failing that, the extent of superpower opposition has been weighed to see whether some other form of operation could be launched. Actions such as UNTEA and Yemen, in which the superpowers acquiesced and where the "involved" nations split the costs; or Cyprus, where the costs were paid by voluntary contributions, probably indicate the trend of peace-keeping operations in the future.

To many observers, the inability of the world's majority to vote peace-keeping measures on a basis of collective responsibility seems a tragic setback for the world organization. On the other hand, it may simply be a recognition of reality. If the fight over Article

19 had been made and won by the United States, the General Assembly would have been given the power to tax its members for peace-keeping operations by a two-thirds vote. The USSR was unalterably opposed to this, and the United States, despite its support of the Uniting for Peace Resolution, the UNEF and ONUC assessments, and the World Court's Advisory Opnion, has since developed serious reservations. Control of the Assembly had now moved into the hands of the Afro-Asian nations. It is interesting to note in this regard that, throughout the 1964-1965 debate on financing, the United States did not seek a vote on the merits of the USSR's constitutional case and, in fact, went to great lengths to provide ways in which the Soviet Union could pay its debt but keep open the constitutional question about the Assembly's powers of assessment. Once again, the superpowers, despite their opposing positions, realized that they had certain interests in common. This partial community of interests has been underlined since 1965 by the tacit agreement of the superpowers to conduct most of their peace-keeping business through the forum of the Security Council. To some extent, Moscow's view of yesterday has become Washington's view today. Certainly, American and Soviet views on peace-keeping have increasingly emphasized the need for political consensus.

In the final analysis, one must see the financial crisis and the subsequent constitutional and political dilemmas as another of the periodic times of consolidation that mark the growth of all political institutions. From their origins in the mid-nineteenth century, international organizations have grown in fits and starts. The United Nations, like its predecessors, will have periods of rapid growth and periods of consolidation. The prophets of doom tend to overlook this time dimension. They pronounce the United Nations dead at a fixed point in time, but ignore the *overall* trend, which is clearly in the direction of a dynamic and evolutionary concept of the process of international organization.

Economic and Social Operations

One of the major purposes of Part III was to test David Mitrany's functionalist thesis that increased contact between the superpowers in practical tasks would lead to better understanding in other fields

—or that superpowers who played together in economic and social matters would stay together in more controversial military and political matters. The limited sample of three cases examined here does not encourage much hope for this thesis.

One can plot U.S.-Soviet behavior in the IRO, the IAEA, and the Special Fund at three points along a spectrum of cooperation. In the IRO, contact between the superpowers never moved beyond the negotiation stage, for their discussions convinced the superpowers that their objectives were too opposed for them to cooperate in the same organization. In the IAEA, the superpowers moved a step beyond negotiations and actually joined the same organization. Yet, the end result was the same: first the United States, then the Soviet Union, decided that they could work more effectively alone than together. In the Special Fund, the superpowers had coexisted within the same agency for several years, but when a point of vital national interest arose, the United States would have upset the proceedings if it could have mustered the votes. In short, the superpowers had the opportunity to meet each other on three different and increasingly intimate levels, but these experiences did not change their views of each other or the primacy accorded to their national interests.

Indeed, our three case studies suggest that the functionalist thesis might be inverted. Political harmony does not seem to depend upon prior economic cooperation. Rather, the success of cooperative economic projects seems itself to depend on a minimum of preexistent political harmony or sympathy between the superpowers' national interests. The assumption that the more potential enemies have contact with one another the better they will understand each other is only partly true. The difficulty is that they may understand better what they dislike and distrust about each other. Realistic knowledge of one's opponent does not guarantee that national interests will become more compatible.

What becomes clear from these three cases is that the superpowers' national interest controls their behavior in economic and social operations, just as it does in other fields.

In the IRO case, the United States used its majority power to create an institution that reflected poorly on the Soviet bloc. The USSR first attacked the proposed agency, then refused to join it.

When by 1952 most of IRO's original wards—primarily from Communist countries—were resettled, the United States limited its financial support and brought the agency to a standstill. The United States also took the initiative in proposing the IAEA, and during the negotiations the superpowers, in their common roles as atomic-producer powers, found themselves sharing a partial community of interest. Yet, once the IAEA was founded, the United States, under pressure from the Congress, by-passed the Agency in order to capitalize on the benefits of bilateral agreements. The USSR followed suit and, in addition, began a competitive debasement process in inspection standards that was reversed only when the IAEA was resuscitated in the context of the nonproliferation treaty. In the Special Fund case, the United States was prepared to upset the concensus principle and attack a project in Cuba, but lacked the votes to do so. Thus, the three cases run the entire spectrum of superpower reactions: from enthusiastic support, through indifference and by-passing, to outright hostility.

What seems clear is that the superpowers had no preconceived attitudes toward economic and social operations as a whole, but determined their positions in each case in accordance with the national interest as they perceived it at the time. The primacy of the national interest emerges particularly clearly in the case of the United States, which terminated the IRO, by-passed the IAEA, attacked the Special Fund, yet supported a host of other economic and social programs. The American sacrifice of international activity to the national interest is as clear in economic and social affairs as the Soviet Union's similar attitude in the realm of peace-keeping. A brief comparison between superpower attitudes in these two fields is relevant at this point.

In the first place, both peace-keeping operations and economic and social operations require a certain amount of superpower support to be launched. A project may be started with consensus, as was the case with ONUC and the IAEA. Or, if one superpower has reservations but the other is enthusiastic, the latter may assume more of the responsibility for the program. UNEF and IRO are cases in point. Second, both types of programs must sustain a minimum of superpower support in order to stay alive. In both fields the number, power, and vehemence of an operation's enemies are more important than the fact that it has enemies. Thus, the extent of active support necessary to sustain an operation in either field will vary with the nature of the opposition. For example, the IRO damaged the national interest of one superpower very badly, but because it served the interest of the other superpower very well, it lived long enough to resettle more than one million refugees. What seems certain, however, is that an operation must retain the support of at least one superpower if it is to remain active. The IRO and IAEA both fell into neglect when neither superpower showed an interest in sustaining these operations. At times, ONUC may have come close to that fate, but, as we saw earlier, that operation had acquired a degree of independent momentum that helped tide it over the worst periods. It is doubtful, however, that either an economic and a social operation or a peace-keeping operation could continue against the opposition of both superpowers, regardless of its momentum. Such an operation would probably have to curtail its activities down to its political consensus. What sustains superpower support in either a peace-keeping operation or an economic and social operation is not necessarily its contribution to a safer or more prosperous world; it is service to the national interest.

A third interesting parallel between peace-keeping operations and economic and social operations may be drawn on the nature of the decision-making process. At the outset of an economic and social project, the United States usually tries to abide by the unanimity principle, which is analogous to using the Security Council on peace-keeping matters. When this technique fails, it resorts to majority voting, as it did in the IRO, at key points in the IAEA negotiation, and would have liked to in the Special Fund case. This technique is analogous to taking a peace-keeping issue to the General Assembly.

If we push the analogy one step further, one sees that the United States takes different positions in the two fields on the matter of superpower financial responsibility. When the USSR opposed an economic and social project, the United States did not press it to assume financial obligations. In the case of the IRO—a Western-dominated agency—there was no American expectation that the Soviet Union would share the bill. Similarly, in the Special Fund dispute, the Congress urged the American delegation to press for a separate vote and to withhold financial support from the project because it injured the national interest. On the other hand, in peace-keeping operations, which can present a far greater danger to the national interest, the United States did insist that the Soviet Union make some payment. In UNEF and, particularly, in ONUC, the United States did press the Soviet Union to finance a project that the latter repeatedly defined as inimical to its national interest. It is interesting that the United States accorded practical recognition to the Soviet Union's national interest in economic and social operations by permitting the USSR to withdraw from and not pay for projects it disliked, while in peace-keeping operations, where national-interest considerations were more sensitive and vital, the principle of collective responsibility was more rigidly applied.

The superpower struggle was extended to economic and social operations. There is no doubt that the entry of the cold war into this field damaged some of the UN's programs. The IAEA was an obvious case in point. Yet, on balance, the evidence suggests that the superpower struggle in this area, as in the other two, has benefited most UN activities. The Soviet Union and its allies became moderate contributors to the UN's development and welfare budgets, and the underdeveloped nations gained in the process. In the case of the IRO, which operated without the Soviet Union, one could argue that the organization might have lasted longer had it not been for the cold war. But one can argue with equal force that the refugee problem would not have received the attention it did in the first place in the United Nations if the majority of refugees had not been fugitives from Communism. On the whole, economic and social programs have grown steadily year after year, with both superpowers paying their shares with a minimum of grumbling.

The Superpowers and the Future of the United Nations

"The crisis of our loyalty to the United Nations," the late Ambassador Adlai E. Stevenson said, "is still ahead of us." When the United States enjoyed an automatic voting majority within the

United Nations, it was not hesitant to identify UN majorities with its national interest, because the two were usually synonymous. It was even willing to undermine the safeguards given to the great powers at San Francisco by circumventing the veto power with the Uniting for Peace Resolution and relying on majority diplomacy. For some time, the belief that UN majorities and the American national interest were congruent seemed justified. During that period, the United States frequently used its voting power to obtain decisions against the Soviet national interest and enforce them in the name of the United Nations.

Today the General Assembly has a majority of developing countries and is dominated in particular by the Afro-Asian group. While the United States has been remarkably successful in avoiding major setbacks thus far, it seems unlikely that the close correlation between UN decisions and the American national interest will continue undisturbed. At some point, the U.S. interest as a Western, highly developed, and anti-Communist state will conflict with the interests of the developing nations, which are more concerned with economic progress and anticolonialism than with Communism. The different attitudes toward Communist Chinese membership in the United Nations illustrates a possible point of future conflict. The case of the Special Fund may also be prophetic. An economically unimportant agricultural project became a *cause célèbre* within the American government and only the total lack of UN support for the American position prevented the destruction of the consensus principle of the Fund. The question arises: What would happen if the United States faced a Special Fund situation in the peace-keeping field? How would the United States react to a UN peace-keeping force mounted to suppress a more successful Bay of Pigs operation? If the Afro-Asian majority, backed by the Soviet Union, passed it over American objections, would the United States pay for it?

The financial crisis and the question of applying sanctions against members refusing to support peace-keeping projects antithetical to their national interests may precipitate the American crisis of loyalty sooner rather than later. In August 1964, the Congress recorded in a 351-0 vote that it was in the American national interest to apply sanctions against recalcitrant members. The implications of this position for future peace-keeping operations, now that the days of automatic pro-U.S. majorities are over, are most serious. If one believes that the United States will never, or at least should never, be in a position in which its national interest conflicts with UN standards, then a rigid attitude on sanctions is defensible. But if one sees the American position in certain economic and social operations as indicative of trends in other areas or believes that the Afro-Asian majority might use its majority power as effectively as the United States did in certain circumstances, then the preservation of some latitude may be desirable.

The Congressional resolution on financing points up another problem peculiar to American relations with the United Nations: the importance of the Congressional view of the national interest and the fact that it does not always agree with that of the Executive. The Congressional view has been an important determinant of American policy in several key cases: the attack on the Secretariat in 1952; the exclusion of Communist China; the reduction in contributions to the IRO; by-passing the IAEA; the attack on the Special Fund; and the pressure to apply sanctions against members defaulting on their peace-keeping assessments. In each case, the Congress fought for what it believed to be the national interest. Its position close to the American public and its responsibility to the electorate have made it understandably sensitive to the more immediate U.S. interests. But it is an open question whether America's *ultimate* interest is better served by continuing to exclude Communist China from the family of nations, or by taking her in. Was it necessary to attack the UN Secretariat so vehemently in order to eliminate possible security risks? And was it better to negotiate uninspected bilateral atomic energy agreements rather than to work with the Soviet Union in the IAEA? It seems likely that the Congress will play a major role in the crisis of loyalty whenever it comes, and that it will favor a position that has in view the immediate benefits to the American national interest.

Our analysis of American behavior in the United Nations in three major fields reveals that the United States does not have a single undifferentiated philosophical approach toward the international organization. From the nine case studies it is clear that the United States reacts to specific situations in a pragmatic manner. It does not tailor its national interests to fit a general philosophy toward the United Nations, but adjusts its "philosophy" to its national interests. When the national interest dictates a larger role for the United Nations, the United States favors expanding the roles of the General Assembly and the Secretary-General, urges major peace-keeping operations, and sustains costly economic and social programs. On the other hand, when the American interest dictates a more conservative role for the United Nations, the United States has employed the hidden veto, attacked the Secretariat, prolonged the membership stalemate, fought for the exclusion of Red China, withdrawn support from the IRO, by-passed the IAEA, and attacked the consensus principle of the Special Fund.

Like the U.S. position, the Soviet Union's attitude toward the United Nations is more easily understood in terms of the national interest rather than as an abstract philosophical position. When the United Nations endangered the Soviet national interests, the USSR attacked the attempts to circumvent its vetoes, opposed an increased role for the General Assembly and the Secretariat, attacked the peace-keeping operation in the Congo, refused to join the IRO, and virtually ignored the IAEA. But on certain occasions, the Soviet national interest dictated a larger role for the United Nations, as in 1956 in Suez against Britain and France and in 1967 against Israel, in the Congo to help Lumumba against Belgium, and in the Special Fund on behalf of Cuba. The fact that the United States has been associated with expanding the role of the United Nations more often than the USSR tells more about the relative voting strengths of the two superpowers than about their philosophies toward the organization.

If we turn from a consideration of the superpowers to the future of the United Nations itself, it becomes clear that, for the time being, the organization is condemned to live between two giants in international politics and to be used or abused by each according to the service it renders the national interest. Yet, if the United Nations is to remain relevant in world politics, it must remain in this position and serve enough of the superpowers' interests for them to choose to deal with it rather than to ignore or crush it. Serving two masters with frequently antithetical interests is no easy task. In this dilemma, the practice of flexible diplomacy, evolved into a fine art by the UN Secretary-General, has stood the Organization in good stead.

The United Nations has demonstrated this flexible diplomacy in at least four major ways. First, it has reinterpreted the Charter on a number of occasions, even inverting it by excluding the superpowers from actual participation in peace-keeping operations. Second, it has shifted the locus of power within the Organization between the Security Council, the General Assembly, and the Secretariat in order to function more effectively. Third, it has financed its operations by a wide variety of means: assessment, voluntary contributions, or the splitting of costs between benefiting parties. Finally, the Secretary-General has tried to guide the course of operations in such a manner that a minimum of political consensus would be maintained and not too many enemies be made at the same time.

Finally, the dominant role of the national interest in the superpowers' policies in the United Nations has not been, and need not become, an insurmountable obstacle to the growth of the Organization. Needless to say, if the superpowers had never been in conflict, many, though not all, of the UN's problems would be eased, and the work and development of the international organization would perhaps be further advanced. The superpower struggle has not been a blessing for the United Nations, but it has not made a meaningful life impossible. Provided the United Nations remains flexible, it should be able to provide some service to both superpowers. And provided the United Nations continues to serve, it can continue to grow. The fact of the matter is that if the superpowers want to use the United Nations in their national interest either against each other or in any other matter, they must first give the Organization sufficient strength to act. This strength, once given, cannot always be entirely recalled. And at times, as we have seen, the United Nations has supplemented this delegated strength with a momentum of its own.

Thus, in 1946, the outbreak of the superpower struggle dashed many hopes that the United Nations would participate meaningfully in international politics. Yet today, by a unique and pragmatic course, the United Nations has carved out for itself a significant role to play between the superpowers. It has had to learn to live between the giants and, ultimately, to capitalize on that position. In this sense, the United Nations has moved forward *because* of the superpower struggle as well as in spite of it.

It has often been said that between the two great chess players —the Soviet Union and the United States—the United Nations is a pawn. There is truth in this assertion. But perhaps the past twenty-five years have shown another truth: that if the United Nations is a pawn, it is being permitted by the superpowers slowly to advance across the board. It will not reach the eighth rank in our time, but it does have certain earmarks of a queen.

SELECTED BIBLIOGRAPHY

Boyd, Andrew. *United Nations: Piety, Myth, and Truth.* London: Penguin Books Ltd., 1962.

Claude, Inis L., Jr. *Swords into Plowshares,* third edition. New York: Random House, 1964.

————. *The Changing United Nations.* New York: Random House, 1967.

Cox, Arthur M. *Prospects for Peacekeeping.* Washington, D.C.: The Brookings Institution, 1967.

Gardner, Richard N. *In Pursuit of World Order.* New York: Praeger, 1964.

Goodrich, Leland M. *The United Nations.* New York: Crowell, 1959.

Russell, Ruth B. *The United Nations and United States Security Policy.* Washington, D.C.: The Brookings Institution, 1968.

Stoessinger, John G. *The Might of Nations: World Politics in Our Time,* third edition. New York: Random House, 1969.

Young, Oran. *The Intermediaries.* Princeton, N.J.: Princeton University Press, 1967.

NOTES

Chapter 1
The Security Council: The Veto and the Superpowers

1 In the "direct-confrontation" category, 7 Soviet vetoes stuck: the Atomic Energy Commission, 325th meeting, June 22, 1948; the CCA (Committee on Conventional Armaments) Work Program, 450th meeting, October 11, 1949; Arms Census Agreement, 452nd meeting, October 18, 1949 (2); election of Secretary-General, 613th meeting, March 13, 1953; Arctic Inspection Proposal, 817th meeting, May 2, 1958. Eight Soviet vetoes were circumvented: reappointment of a Secretary-General, 510th meeting, October 12, 1950; the Hungarian crisis, 754th meeting, November 4, 1956; the Congo crisis, 906th meeting, September 16, 1960; the Congo crisis, 920th meeting, December 12-13, 1960; the Congo crisis, 942nd meeting, February 20-21, 1961 (2); the Congo crisis, 982nd meeting, November 24, 1961 (2); the Czechoslovak crisis, 1443rd meeting, August 23, 1968.

Three Soviet vetoes were bypassed either by direct negotiations between the disputants or by outside events: the Berlin Blockade, 372nd meeting, October 25, 1948; the U.S. RB-47 incident, 883rd meeting, July 26, 1960 (2).

2 In the "veto-cast-for-an-ally" category, the Soviet vetoes stuck: the Czechoslovakia case, 303rd meeting, May 24, 1948 (2).

Eleven vetoes were circumvented: Greek Civil War, 70th meeting, September 20, 1946; Greek Civil War, 170th meeting, July 29, 1947; Greek Civil War, 188th meeting, August 19, 1947 (2); Greek Civil War, 202nd meeting, September 15, 1947 (2); the Korean War, 496th meeting, September 6, 1950; the Korean War, 501st meeting, September 12, 1950; the Korean War, 530th meeting, November 30, 1950; the Korean War (Germ Warfare), 587th meeting, July 3, 1952; the Korean War (Germ Warfare), 590th meeting, July 9, 1952.

Three Soviet vetoes were superseded: Corfu Channel Case, 122nd meeting, March 25, 1947; Infiltration in Indochina, 674th meeting, March 29, 1954; Guatemalan coup, 675th meeting, June 20, 1954.

3 Seven of the Soviet proxy vetoes stuck: Palestine-Jordan River Diversion, 656th meeting, January 22, 1954; Kashmir, 773rd meeting, February 20, 1957; Goa, 988th meeting, December 18-19, 1961; Israeli-Syrian dispute, August 3, 1963; Malaysian-Indonesian dispute, September 16, 1964; Syrian-Israeli dispute, December 21, 1964; Syrian-Israeli dispute, November 4, 1966.

Six of the Soviet "vetoes by proxy" were circumvented: Indonesia, 456th meeting, December 13, 1949 (2); Suez Canal shipping, 664th meeting, March 29, 1954; Suez Canal nationalization crisis, 743rd meeting, October 13, 1956; Lebanon, 834th meeting, July 18, 1958; Lebanon, 837th meeting, July 22, 1958.

Three of the vetoes were bypassed: Syria-Lebanon case, 23rd meeting, February 16, 1946; Kuwait, 960th meeting, July 7, 1961; Kashmir, 1016th meeting, June 22, 1962.

4 Eight of the membership vetoes have stuck: South Korea, 423rd meeting, April 8, 1949; South Vietnam, 603rd meeting, September 9, 1952; South Korea, 704th meeting, December 13, 1955; South Vietnam, 704th meeting, December 13, 1955; South Korea, 790th meeting, September 9, 1957; South Vietnam, 790th meeting, September 9, 1957; South Korea, 843rd meeting, December 9, 1958; South Vietnam, 843rd meeting, December 9, 1958.

Forty-three of the membership vetoes were bypassed: Trans-Jordan, Portugal, Ireland, 57th meeting, August 29, 1946; Trans-Jordan, Ireland, Portugal, 186th meeting, August 18, 1947; Italy and Austria, 190th meeting, August 21, 1947; Italy and Finland, 206th meeting, October 1, 1947; Italy, 279th meeting, April 10, 1948; Ceylon, 351st meeting, August 18, 1948; Ceylon, 384th meeting, December 15, 1948; Nepal, 439th meeting, September 7, 1949; Portugal, Jordan, Italy, Finland, Ireland, Austria, Ceylon, 443rd meeting, September 13, 1949; Italy, 573rd meeting, February 6, 1952; Libya, 600th meeting, September 16, 1952; Japan, 602nd meeting, September 18, 1952; Laos and Cambodia, 603rd meeting, September 19, 1952; Jordan, Ireland, Portugal, Italy, Austria, Finland, Ceylon, Nepal, Libya, Cambodia, Japan, Laos, Spain, 704th meeting, December 13, 1955; Japan, 705th meeting, December 14, 1955; Japan, 706th meeting, December 15, 1955; Mauritania, 911th meeting, December 3-4, 1960; Kuwait, 985th meeting, December 18-19, 1961.

5 The Spanish case, 47th meeting, June 18, 1946; the Spanish case, 49th meeting, June 26, 1946 (3).

6 The Spanish case (France and USSR), 49th meeting, June 26, 1946; Indonesian question (France), 194th meeting, August 25, 1947; Membership of Mongolia (China), 704th meeting, December 13, 1955; Palestine-Suez crisis (France and United Kingdom), 749th meeting, October 30, 1956; Palestine-Suez crisis (France and United Kingdom), 750th meeting, October 30, 1956; Southern Rhodesia (United Kingdom), August, 1963.

7 Cited by Inis L. Claude, Jr., *Swords, into Plowshares*, third edition (New York: Random House, 1964), p. 135.

8 Cited by Arthur N. Holcombe, "The Role of Politics in the Organization of Peace," in his *Organizing Peace in the Nuclear Age* (New York: New York University Press, 1959), p. 97.

9 Norman J. Padelford, "The Use of the Veto," *International Organization* (June 1948), pp. 231-232.

10 Andrew Boyd, *United Nations: Piety, Myth, and Truth* (London: Penguin Books, 1962), pp. 32-33.

11 *Ibid.*

Chapter 2
The General Assembly:
The Problem of Membership and the China Puzzle

1 Advisory Opinion of the International Court of Justice on Condition of Admission of New Members to the United Nations, May 28, 1948. International Court of Justice, *Reports of Judgements, Advisory Opinions and Orders*, 1948, pp. 57-66.

2 Leland M. Goodrich, *The United Nations* (New York: Crowell, 1959), p. 100.

3 UN Doc. S/1466; Security Council, *Official Records*, Fifth year, Supplement 4, January 1–May 31, 1950.

4 Cited in Goodrich, *op. cit.*, p. 101.

5 *Swords into Plowshares* (New York: Random House, 1959), p. 104. (Italics Claude's.)

6 Cited in H. Arthur Steiner, "Communist China in the World Community," *International Conciliation*, No. 533 (May 1961), pp. 389-454.

7 *New York Times* (July 9, 1954). Cited by Claude, *op. cit.*, p. 105.

8 Testimony of Mr. Dulles on January 18, 1954, *Charter Review Hearing*, Part I, pp. 7, 13, 18, 20. Cited by Claude, *op. cit.*, p. 106.

9 Steiner, *op. cit.*, p. 447.

10 Address by Adlai Stevenson, delegate of the United States to the Sixteenth General Assembly, December 1, 1961. In Richard P. Stebbins, ed., *Documents on American Foreign Relations* (New York: Harper and Bros. for the Council on Foreign Relations, 1961), p. 499.

11 *The United Nations Review* (November 1962), p. 33.

12 *Ibid.*, p. 32.

13 *Ibid.*, p. 33.

Chapter 3
The Secretary-General:
The American and Soviet Attacks on the Secretariat,
1952 and 1960

1 Cited in Wilder Foote, ed., *Dag Hammarskjöld, Servant of Peace: A Selection of His Speeches and Statements* (New York: Harper & Row, 1962), p. 351.

2 Cited by H. C. Nicholas, *The United Nations as a Political Institution* (New York: Oxford University Press, 1959), p. 153.

3 Report of the Secretary-General on Personnel Policy, January 30, 1953, UN Doc. A/2364, p. 19.

4 *Ibid.*, p. 10.

5 *Ibid.*

6 Trygve Lie, *In the Cause of Peace* (New York: The Macmillan Company, 1954), p. 388.

7 *Ibid.*, pp. 395-96.

8 *Ibid.*, p. 397.

9 *New York Times* (December 1, 1952).

10 *Ibid.* (December 3, 1952).

11 Lie, *op. cit.*, pp. 400-01.

12 UN Doc. A/2364, *op. cit.*, p. 10.

13 *Ibid.*, p. 55.

14 Report of the Secretary-General on Personnel Policy (November 21, 1953), UN Doc. A/2533, p. 17.

15 *Ibid.*

16 The vote was 41 to 6, with the United States and 12 other members abstaining. Res. 785, VIII (December 9, 1953).

17 "Effect of Awards of Compensation Made by the U.N. Administrative Tribunal, Advisory Opinion of July 13th, 1954," *ICJ Reports* (1954), p. 47.

18 Richard P. Stebbins, ed., *The U.S. in World Affairs* (New York: Harper and Bros. for the Council on Foreign Relations, 1953), p. 398.

19 House Congressional Res. 262, 83rd Congress (August 20, 1954).

20 *New York Times* (October 17, 1954).

21 Inis L. Claude, Jr., *Swords into Plowshares,* third edition (New York: Random House, 1964), p. 187.

22 Lie, *op. cit.*, p. 404.

23 Draft Resolution submitted to the Security Council by Tunisia and Ceylon on September 16, 1960 (S/4523); defeated on September 17 by a vote of 8 to 2 (USSR and Poland), with France abstaining.

24 For a more complete discussion and analysis of the UN in the Congo, see Chapter 6.

25 Address by Premier Nikita Khrushchev to the General Assembly, September 23, 1960; cited in Richard P. Stebbins, ed., *Documents on American Foreign Relations, 1960* (New York: Harper and Bros. for the Council on Foreign Relations), pp. 563-69.

26 *New York Times* (September 27, 1960).

27 Text of the Soviet Government's Statement on the Death of Patrice Lumumba, February 14, 1961, in Richard P. Stebbins, ed., *Documents on American Foreign Relations, 1961* (New York: Harper and Bros. for the Council on Foreign Relations), pp. 337-40.

28 Statement to the Security Council, February 15, 1961; *New York Times* (February 16, 1961).

29 Alexander Dallin, *The Soviet Union at the United Nations* (New York: Frederick A. Praeger, 1962), p. 205.

30 Address by President Kennedy to the General Assembly, September 25, 1961, in Richard P. Stebbins, ed., *Documents on American Foreign Relations, 1961* (New York: Harper and Bros. for the Council on Foreign Relations), pp. 473-84.

31 Dallin, *op. cit.*, p. 176.

Chapter 4

The Middle East Crises of 1956 and 1967 and the United Nations Emergency Force

1 *Full Circle: The Memoirs of Anthony Eden,* cited by Herbert Feis in *Foreign Affairs* (July 1960), p. 600.

2 UN Doc. S/3712 (October 29, 1956).

3 UN Security Council, *Official Records,* 11th Year, 750th Meeting (October 31, 1956).

4 *Ibid.*, 755th Meeting (November 5, 1956).

5 "Radio and Television Address by President Eisenhower, October 31, 1956," in U.S. Department of State, *United States Policy in the Middle East,* p. 49.

6 "Statement in the UN General Assembly by Secretary of State Dulles (November 1, 1956)," *ibid.*, pp. 151-57.

7 UN General Assembly, *Official Records,* 1st Emergency Special Session, 562nd Meeting (November 1, 1956), p. 18.

8 *Ibid.*, p. 36.

9 UN General Assembly, *Official Records,* 563rd Meeting (November 3, 1956), pp. 55-71.

10 UN Doc. A/3290 (November 4, 1956).

11 Dean Acheson, *Power and Diplomacy* (Cambridge, Mass.: Harvard University Press, 1958), pp. 109-16.

12 Inis L. Claude, Jr., *Swords into Plowshares,* second edition (New York: Random House, 1959), p. 460.

13 UN General Assembly, *Official Records,* 1st Emergency Special Session, 567th Meeting (November 7, 1956), pp. 127-28.

14 Lester Pearson, "Force for UN," *Foreign Affairs,* XXXV (April 1957), p. 401.

Chapter 5
The Congo Crisis
and the United Nations Operation in the Congo

1 *New York Times* (July 10, 1960).
2 *Ibid.* (July 24, 1960).
3 *Ibid.*
4 UN Doc. S/4426 (August 9, 1960).
5 UN Press Release GA/AB/842 (May 22, 1963).
6 Interview with Dr. Andrew W. Cordier (March 18, 1963).
7 UN Doc. S/4526 (September 17, 1960).
8 GAOR, 4th Emergency Special Session, 858th Plenary Meeting (September 17, 1960).
9 General Assembly Res. 1474 (ES-IV) (September 20, 1960).
10 UN Doc. S/4741 (February 21, 1961).
11 UN Doc. S/PV 982 (November 24, 1961), pp. 71-75.

Chapter 6
The United Nations Financial Crisis
and the Superpowers

1 UN General Assembly, *Official Records* (GAOR), Eleventh Session, Fifth Committee, 541st Meeting (December 3, 1956), par. 79.
2 GAOR, Fifteenth Session, Fifth Committee, 775th Meeting (October 26, 1960), par. 8.
3 UN Doc. A/C.5/843 (November 21, 1960), pp. 1, 8.
4 See GAOR, Fifteenth Session, Annexes, Agenda items 49/50 (A/C.5/860, March 27, 1961), and UN Doc. A/PV.977 (April 5, 1961), p. 11.
5 On October 30, the Assembly authorized the Secretariat to commit up to $10 million a month for the remainder of 1961. However, it left the mode of financing for "later deliberation."
6 These were: Australia, Canada, Central African Republic, Ceylon, Dahomey, Denmark, Finland, Gabon, Iceland, India, Ireland, Ivory Coast, Japan, Liberia, Malaya, Netherlands, New Zealand, Nigeria, Norway, Pakistan, Tunisia, Turkey, United Kingdom, United States.
7 General Assembly Res. 1731, XVI (December 20, 1961). The Resolution was sponsored by the United States, Brazil, Cameroon, Canada, Denmark, Japan, United Kingdom, Liberia, Sweden, and Pakistan.

Chapter 7
Human Rights: The International Refugee Organization

1 Verbatim Records of the Meetings of the Third Committee of the General Assembly (January 28, 1946).

2 *Ibid.* (February 8, 1946).

3 *New York Times* (February 2, 1946).

4 Verbatim Records (February 3, 1946).

5 UN Doc. E/Ref. 1, p. 35.

6 Verbatim Records (February 4, 1946).

7 UN Doc. E/Ref. 1.

8 UN Doc. A/C/#/12, p. 5, Annex H.

9 Verbatim Records (February 4, 1946).

10 *Ibid.* (February 7, 1946).

11 UN Docs. E/Ref. 1 and E/Ref. 75.

12 UN Doc. E/15, Annex A (February 14, 1946).

13 UN Doc. E/Ref. 1.

14 *Ibid.*

15 *Ibid.*

16 *Ibid.*

17 UN Doc. E/Ref. 75, Addendum 1.

18 *Ibid.*

19 *Ibid.*

20 *Ibid.*

21 UN Docs. E/87 and E/92 (February 6, 1946).

22 UN Doc. A/C/2/23.

23 UN Doc. E/Ref. 1.

24 UN Doc. E/Ref. 75.

25 UN Doc. E/Ref. 1.

26 Verbatim Records (February 9, 1946).

27 *Ibid.*

28 *Ibid.*

29 UN Doc. E/15 (February 14, 1946).

30 UN Doc. E/Ref. 75.

31 Verbatim Records (February 10, 1946).

32 *Ibid.*

33 *Pro:* Australia, Belgium, United Kingdom, United States, Netherlands, Canada, Denmark, Philippines, South Africa, France, Panama, Egypt, New Zealand.
   Con: USSR, Byelorussia, Ukraine, Poland, Yugoslavia.
   Abstaining: Czechoslovakia, Lebanon, Iraq.

34 *New York Times* (February 13, 1946).

35 *Pravda* (February 13, 1946).

36 UN Doc. A/C/3/23 (March 1, 1946).

37 UN Doc. E/Ref. 1.

38 UN Doc. A/C/3/23 (March 1, 1946).

39 For a detailed discussion of IRO financing see John G. Stoessinger and Associates, *Financing the United Nations System* (Washington, D.C.: The Brookings Institution, 1964), pp. 197-99.

40 UN Doc. Records, General Assembly, Second Session, p. 1453.

41 *Pro:* Belgium, Canada, China, Cuba, Denmark, Dominican Republic, Ecuador, France, Greece, Guatemala, Honduras, Iceland, Iran, Lebanon, Liberia, Luxembourg, Mexico, Netherlands, Nicaragua, Norway, Panama, Paraguay, Peru, Philippines, South Africa, United Kingdom, United States, Uruguay, Venezuela.
Con: USSR, Ukraine, Byelorussia, Yugoslavia, Poland.
Abstaining: Afghanistan, Argentina, Australia, Bolivia, Brazil, Chile, Colombia, Costa Rica, Czechoslovakia, Egypt, Ethiopia, Haiti, India, Iraq, Saudi Arabia, Sweden, Syria, Turkey.

Chapter 8
The International Atomic Energy Agency and the Nonproliferation Treaty

1 "Atomic Power for Peace," address delivered by President Eisenhower before the General Assembly of the United Nations (December 8, 1953).

2 *Ibid.*

3 Bernard G. Bechhoefer and Eric Stein, "Atoms for Peace: The New International Atomic Energy Agency," *Michigan Law Review*, Vol. 55, No. 6 (April 1957), p. 785.

4 For the text of these documents see *Atoms for Peace Manual*, S. Doc. No. 55, 84th Congress, 1st Session (1954), p. 274.

5 *Ibid.*, pp. 269, 271-72.

6 *Ibid.*, p. 278.

7 Memorandum by Assistant Secretary of State Merchant (July 9, 1954), to Ambassador Zarubin: see *Atoms for Peace Manual*, No. 55, p. 276.

8 *Atoms for Peace Manual*, p. 278.

9 Soviet Union Aide Memoire of September 22, 1954, *ibid.*, p. 278.

10 Ninth General Assembly, First Committee, A/C.1/SR. 723 (November 19, 1954).

11 *Ibid.*

12 *Ibid.*

13 Res. 912 (X), Doc. A/3116, in UN General Assembly *Official Records*, 10th Session, Supplement 19, pp. 4-5.

[14] Report of Ambassador Morehead Patterson, 34 Department of State Bulletin, No. 5 (1956).

[15] *Ibid.*

[16] Working Level Meeting on the Draft Statute of the IAEA, Doc. 5 (March 2, 1956).

[17] The eight major regions of the world were defined as North America, Latin America, Western Europe, Eastern Europe, Africa and the Middle East, South Asia, South East Asia and the Pacific, and the Far East.

[18] Report of the Working Level Meeting on the Draft Statute of the International Atomic Energy Agency, Doc. 31 (Washington, D.C., July 2, 1956).

[19] Amendments to that effect were proposed by Egypt, Ethiopia, Indonesia, Philippines, Syria, and Japan. IAEA/CS/OR. 6 (September 26, 1956).

[20] IAEA/CS/OR. 20 (October 3, 1956).

[21] *Ibid.*

[22] *Ibid.*

[23] Working Level Meeting on the Draft Statute of the IAEA, Doc. 5 (March 2, 1956).

[24] *Ibid.*

[25] See IAEA Statute, Art. V, para. F.

[26] *Ibid.*, para. D.

[27] Bechhoefer and Stein, *op. cit.*, p. 753.

[28] Report of the Working Level Meeting on the Draft Statute of the International Atomic Energy Agency, Doc. 31 (Washington, D.C., July 2, 1956).

[29] Working Level Meeting on the Draft Statute of the IAEA; Statement by Ambassador James J. Wadsworth (March 2, 1956).

[30] See IAEA Statute, Art. XII, para. A.

[31] Working Level Meeting, *op. cit.*; Statement by Ambassador Zarubin.

[32] IAEA/GOV/OR. 1 (October 21, 1957).

[33] IAEA/GOV/OR. 74 (June 19, 1958).

[34] *Ibid.*

[35] IAEA Statute, Art. III.

[36] IAEA/GOV/OR. 67 (June 12, 1958).

[37] *Ibid.*

[38] IAEA/GOV/OR. 83 (July 2, 1958).

[39] *Ibid.*

[40] *Ibid.*

[41] *New York Times* (November 13, 1958).

[42] General Assembly Res. 2373 (XXII), (June 12, 1968).

[43] General Assembly Res. 1665 (XVI), (December 4, 1961).

[44] General Assembly Res. 1664 (XVI), (December 4, 1961).

[45] The ENDC is composed of eighteen nations: the United States, Can-

ada, Britain, France, and Italy for the West; the Soviet Union, Poland, Czechoslovakia, Bulgaria, and Rumania for the East; and eight non-aligned countries: Brazil, Burma, Ethiopia, India, Mexico, Nigeria, Sweden, and the UAR.

46 General Assembly Res. 2028 (XX), (November 23, 1965).

47 General Assembly Res. 2373 (XXII), (June 12, 1968). Voting against were Albania, Cuba, Tanzania, and Zambia. Not voting were Cambodia, the Dominican Republic, Gambia, and Haiti. Abstentions were Algeria, Argentina, Brazil, Burma, Burundi, Central African Republic, Congo (Brazzaville), France, Gabon, Guinea, India, Malawi, Mali, Mauritania, Niger, Portugal, Rwanda, Saudi Arabia, Sierra Leone, Spain, and Uganda.

48 Security Council Res. 255 (June 19, 1968). Those abstaining were Algeria, Brazil, France, India, and Pakistan.

Chapter 9
A United Nations Dilemma: Cuba and the Special Fund

1 Statement of Richard N. Gardner to subcommittee of Senate Committee on Foreign Relations, in *Senate Committee on Foreign Relations, Hearings on the Special Fund,* February 18, 1963 (Washington, D.C.: Government Printing Office), p. 2.

2 Statement of Mr. Klutznick to the Government Council of the Special Fund, in *Senate Committee on Foreign Relations, Hearings on the Special Fund,* February 10, 1963 (Washington, D.C.: Government Printing Office), pp. 25 ff.

3 Statement by Richard Gardner, *op. cit.*

4 W. Frye, "UN Approves Aid For Cuba—and Ducks," *Los Angeles Times* (February 17, 1963).

5 Mr. Gardner's testimony, *op. cit.*, p. 37.

6 Frye, *op. cit.*

7 U.S. Department of State Press Release No. 99: *The United Nations in Crisis: Cuba and the Congo* (February 22, 1963), p. 6.

Chapter 10
The United Nations and the Superpowers

1 *New York Times,* Magazine Section (March 14, 1965), p. 37.

INDEX